SO-AYF-776

JBIO
ALHAYTHAM

Ibn al-Haytham: First Scientist

Ibn al-Haytham:
First Scientist

Bradley Steffens

MORGAN
REYNOLDS
PUBLISHING
Greensboro, North Carolina

Profiles
IN SCIENCE

Robert Boyle

Rosalind Franklin

Ibn al-Haytham

Edmond Halley

Marie Curie

Antonio Meucci

Caroline Herschel

IBN AL-HAYTHAM: FIRST SCIENTIST

Copyright © 2007 by Bradley Steffens

Library of Congress Cataloging-in-Publication Data

Steffens, Bradley, 1955-
  Ibn al-Haytham : first scientist / Bradley Steffens. -- 1st ed.
     p. cm.
  Includes bibliographical references and index.
  ISBN-13: 978-1-59935-024-0 (lib. bdg.)
  ISBN-10: 1-59935-024-6 (lib. bdg.)
  1. Alhazen, 965-1039. 2. Scientists--Iraq--Biography. I. Title.
Q143.A46S74 2006
509.2--dc22
[B]
                                          2006023970

Printed in the United States of America
First Edition

To Bryan and Brayden Steffens,
who were born as this book came into being

Contents

Chapter One
Boyhood in Basra   11

Chapter Two
Scholar of Basra   27

Chapter Three
"Madness"   39

Chapter Four
To Egypt   47

Chapter Five
Scholar of Cairo   57

Chapter Six
Return to Basra   76

Chapter Seven
"The Physicist"   91

Timeline   117

Sources   118

Bibliography   123

Web sites   125

Index   126

Ibn al-Haytham. (University of Cairo)

ONE

Boyhood in Basra

At the beginning of *Kitab al-Manazir*, or *The Book of Optics*, the medieval scholar Ibn al-Haytham expresses skepticism about the ability of human beings to understand the complex workings of nature. "When inquiry concerns subtle matters, perplexity grows, views diverge, opinions vary, conclusions differ, and certainty becomes difficult to obtain," he wrote. One of the problems with discovering the truth about nature, Ibn al-Haytham realized, is that human beings have physical limitations that can affect their observations. "The premises are gleaned from the senses," he wrote, "and the senses, which are our tools, are not immune from error."

Haunted by doubts about human perception and reason, Ibn al-Haytham searched for new ways to establish the validity of observations, theories, and conclusions.

Knowing that mathematical equations and geometric proofs did not vary from person to person, he used mathematics to describe natural phenomena whenever possible. He also devised simple, repeatable experiments to test hypotheses and support conclusions. By systematically applying these methods of inquiry to his research, Ibn al-Haytham helped to launch a new era in the history of learning—the age of modern science.

The man who revolutionized the practice of science was born in Basra, in what is now Iraq, in 965 A.D. His full name, Abu 'Ali al-Hasan ibn al-Hasan ibn al-Haytham, reveals several important things about him and his family. The name is Arabic, indicating that his ancestors were Arabs, people from the Arabian peninsula. It also shows that they were Muslims, adherents to the religion of Islam. His given name, al-Hasan, was also as his father's name. Al-Haytham was his grandfather's name. Centuries later, when unknown European scholars translated *Kitab al-Manazir* into Latin, they shortened the author's name to al-Hasan, which they wrote as "Alhacen" or "Alhazen." Other Western scholars adopted the same practice when they translated other books by Ibn al-Haytham. The Latinized version of Ibn al-Haytham's name became so ingrained in Western society that even today most libraries list books by and about the Arab scientist under "Alhazen."

Ibn al-Haytham's ancestors were part of a mass migration of Arabs that began around 630 and continued for hundreds of years. Following the teachings of the founder of Islam, Muhammad ibn 'Abd Allah ibn 'Abd

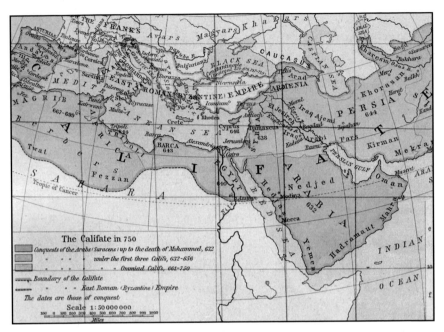

United under the Umayyad dynasty, territory under Islamic control stretched to its furthest extent in the year 750. (University of Texas)

al-Muttalib, also known as the Prophet Muhammad, Arab Muslims swept out of Arabia and conquered many neighboring lands, including Iraq. Within one hundred years, the Arab Muslim empire stretched from Spain in the West to India in the East.

The Arab Muslims did not mix with the people they conquered. Their goal was to rule the native populations and collect taxes from them. After conquering Iraq, the Muslims occupied the northern city of Mosul, making it the seat of their new government. They also founded two new cities: Al-Kufah in the center of the country and Basra in the south. These outposts served as regional bases for Muslim rule. The Muslim warriors, their families, and waves of Arab immigrants settled in these new cities.

Although the Arab Muslims remained apart from the local people, they did not shun the native cultures. On the contrary, they were eager to absorb the knowledge of their subjects. This thirst for knowledge partly sprang from the religious philosophy of Islam, which exhorts the faithful to learn as much as possible about the universe. "Those who remember Allah [God] . . . reflect on the creation of the heavens and the earth," declares the Qur'an, the holy book of the Muslims. The Prophet Muhammad declared, "Seeking knowledge is a duty upon every Muslim."

The Muslims were particularly interested in the writings of the ancient Greeks, who had lived along the northern coast of the Mediterranean Sea more than one thousand years earlier. The Greeks, who worshipped a group of gods said to live atop Mount Olympus, the highest peak in Greece, had made many important discoveries in the fields of philosophy, mathematics, medicine, and astronomy. Around 150 B.C., the Greeks were conquered by the Romans, who ruled much of Europe, the Middle East, and northern Africa for another six hundred years. The Romans copied and spread ancient Greek writings—including books by philosophers such as Aristotle and Plato; mathematicians such as Archimedes, Euclid, and Apollonius of Perga; the physician Galen; and the astronomer Ptolemy—throughout the Mediterranean region. Wealthy Muslims paid scholars to translate the works of the ancient Greeks into Arabic.

One of the most active collectors of ancient Greek works was Abu Jafar al-Ma'mun ibn Harun, the caliph, or ruler, of Iraq from 813 to 833. Determined to build one of the

Raphael's School of Athens *at the Stanza della Segnatura, Palazzi Pontifici, Vatican, portrays Plato* (left) *and Aristotle* (right) *under the central arch. Ptolemy, standing in the far right foreground with his back to the observer, holds an earthly sphere. To the left of Ptolemy, leaning down, is either Euclid or Archimedes demonstrating geometry with two compasses and a slate.*

greatest libraries in the Muslim world, Caliph al-Ma'mun founded the Bait-ul-Hikmat, or "House of Wisdom," a center dedicated to the study and translation of books. Scholars at the House of Wisdom translated the works of the ancient Greeks and other non-Muslims, including Persians, Jews, Christians, and Indians. Caliph al-Ma'mun located the House of Wisdom in Madinat al-Salam, or "City of Peace," the new capital of Iraq, which the Muslims had founded in 762 on the site of the village of Baghdad.

Drawn by Caliph al-Ma'mun's generous pay, scholars from as far away as India and Spain traveled to Baghdad, as the new capital came to be called, to work at the House of Wisdom. Scholars did not have to be Muslims in order to translate for Caliph al-Ma'mun. Christians, Jews, Persians, and Indians worked side by side with Muslims to interpret the wisdom of the ancients. For example,

Sahl ibn Rabban al-Tabari, the scholar who translated Ptolemy's astronomical manual, *Mathematike Syntaxis,* or *The Mathematical Arrangement*, into Arabic was a Jew from the city of Marw. Al-Tabari called Ptolemy's great

On Islamic maps, North is always found at the bottom of the page. This tenth century map of northern Iraq shows the Tigris (left) and Euphrates (right). Baghdad is indicated by the bold black writing at the top. (Egyptian National Library, Cairo)

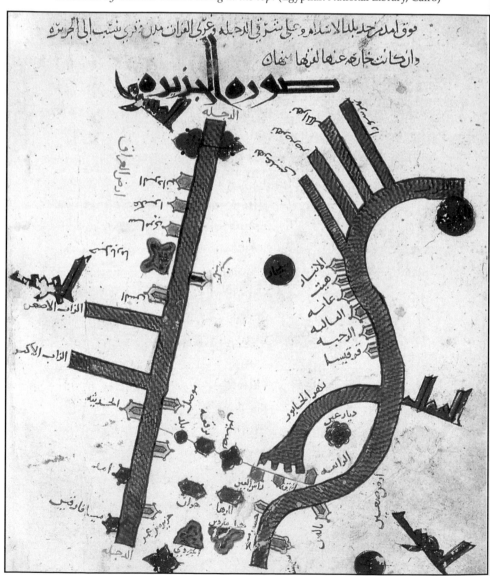

work *al-Majisti* (meaning "The Great Book"), which later was transliterated as *Almagest*. Years later, Ibn al-Haytham worked from al-Tabari's translation of *Mathematike Syntaxis* when he wrote commentaries on Ptolemy's book.

The most famous book to emerge from the golden age of Muslim translation is *Alf Laylah Wa Laylah*, known in the West as *One Thousand and One Arabian Nights*. Early in the tenth century, an Iraqi scholar named Abu 'Abd Allah ibn 'Abdus al-Jashyari began to translate Persian, Indian, Iranian, Turkish, and Chinese stories into Arabic. He gave the heroes of these exotic tales the Arabic names they are known by today, including Aladdin, Ali Baba, Scheherazade, and Sinbad. In some cases, al-Jashyari changed not only the names of the characters but also the locations of their adventures.

After al-Jashyari's death, other Muslim scholars and storytellers continued to add to his collection until it contained the full 1001 stories suggested by the title. According to a medieval Arab chronicler named Abu Al-husayn 'ali Ibn Al-husayn Al-mas'udi, by 947 the collection of stories was "called by the people 'A Thousand Nights'," indicating that the tales were popular in Iraq shortly before Ibn al-Haytham was born. Since al-Jashyari was from Basra, it is likely that Ibn al-Haytham read *One Thousand and One Arabian Nights* as a young man or heard storytellers recite its tales of flying carpets, powerful genies, and magic caves. Ibn al-Haytham left behind no record of ever reading or being influenced by al-Jashyari's book, but within a few years he, like Sinbad, would venture out

Ali Baba's son, who one day invited him to his father's house. On hearing that the new guest would eat no salt with his meat, Morgiana's suspicions were aroused, and she recognised him as the captain of the robbers. After dinner she undertook to perform a dance before the company, and at the end of it pointed a dagger at the captain, and then plunged it into his heart. Ali Baba was very much shocked, until Morgiana explained the reasons for her conduct; he then gave her to his son in marriage, and they lived in great prosperity and happiness ever after.

This illustration of "Ali Baba and the Forty Thieves" comes from Walter Crane's 1872 edition of The Arabian Nights. *Scholars debate whether or not the story was included in al-Jashyari's manuscript or if it was added much later.* (Courtesy of the Granger Collection.)

from Basra to seek fame and fortune among the far-flung outposts of the Arab Empire.

The "Arab Empire," however, was not a single, cohesive political entity. At the time of Ibn al-Haytham's birth, the Baghdad-based Abbasid Caliphate was shrinking and losing power to regional governors, known as amirs, and competing religious sects. Spain, then known as Andalus, had fallen into the hands of the Umayyads, from whom the Abbasids had conquered the eastern caliphate in the eighth century. Another rival, the Fatimid Caliphate, rose in North Africa. The Abbasids faced enemies in the East as well. In 946, less than twenty years before Ibn al-Haytham was born, Baghdad was invaded and occupied by the Shi'ite Persian house of Buyeh. The Persians did not depose the caliph, whose religious title was useful in governing the Sunnah Muslim population, but instead made him their puppet ruler.

Despite the rival political factions, the vast majority of the Middle East was under some sort of Muslim rule, whether it was Arab, Turkish, or Persian. As *One Thousand and One Arabian Nights* suggests, the Muslims did not merely collect and translate the works of other cultures. They absorbed the material and added to it, making it their own. This was true not only in literature, but also in science and mathematics. Muslim advances in these areas changed the course of human history.

The most important breakthrough to come out of the House of Wisdom occurred around 825 when Muhammad ibn Musa al-Khwarizmi, a mathematician and astronomer, came across works by Hindu mathematicians that had been translated into Arabic. The Hindu mathematicians used a numbering system that included ten numerals: 1 through 9, and 0. At the time, most of the world used numbering systems, such as the one developed by the Romans, that did not include a zero as a placeholder. Impressed with the power and economy of the ten-digit, or decimal, numbering system, al-Khwarizmi began to use it in his astronomical calculations. He decided to explain the advantages of the Hindu system in a work he called *The Book of Addition and Subtraction According to the Hindu Calculation.* Adopted by everyone from scholars to merchants, al-Khwarizmi's numbering system swept through the Muslim world and eventually spread through Spain to Europe and beyond. Today the Hindu-Arabic numbering system is used worldwide.

Al-Khwarizmi was responsible for the widespread acceptance of another important concept that also changed the course of mathematics: algebra. This term came from the Latin translation of the Arabic word *al-jabr,* which appears in the title of another of al-Khwarizmi's books, *Al-Kitab al-Mukhtasar fi Hisab al-Jabr Wa'l-muqabala,* or *The Compendious Book on Calculation by Completion and Balancing,* in which al-Khwarizmi described a system of rules that could be used to solve certain mathematical problems. His book inspired another Muslim mathematician, Abu Kamil, who lived from 850 to 930, to create an even more advanced form of algebra. Eventually Abu Kamil's book made its way to Europe where it inspired new generations of mathematicians to expand on his concepts, advancing algebra even further.

Algebra proved to have many practical uses in the Muslim world. It helped Muslim leaders to divide up parcels of land, assess taxes, and distribute inheritances according to

Muslim law. It also helped astronomers calculate the exact time to look for the new moon, marking the beginning of each month on the Muslim calendar. Since Muslims are required to face the city of Mecca when they say their prayers five times a day, they had to know the precise direction of the holy city. Muslim astronomers used algebra to make these important calculations for the faithful.

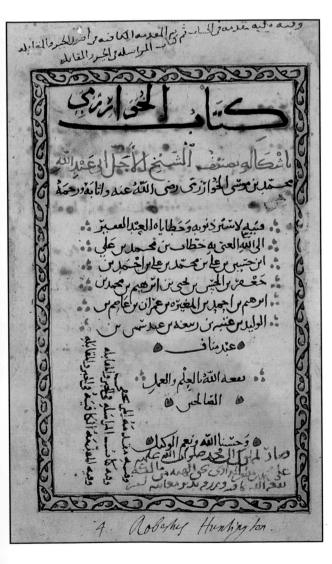

A leaf from al-Khwarizmi's book on algebra. (Bodleian Library, University of Oxford, Oxford)

THE ISLAMIC CALENDAR

The Islamic calendar is used by many Muslims to date historical events and determine the dates of Muslim holy days. The calendar is based on lunar cycles, with twelve lunar months and about 354 days in a year. Each month begins with the first sighting of the *hilal*, or lunar crescent, after sunset. The holiest month in the Islamic year is Ramadan, the ninth month, during which many Muslims fast during the day. Because weather conditions often do not allow for *hilal* sightings, some Muslims today use calendars worked out in advance, but traditionally the month does not officially begin until someone has physically seen the *hilal*. The importance of moon sightings in Islamic culture fueled interest in astronomy.

Pre-Islamic calendars had also used lunar months, but also added an extra month, called an intercalary month, so that one year would coincide with a solar year and the seasons would remain constant. Muhammad, however, expressly forbid the use of an intercalary month. Because an Islamic year is about eleven days shorter than a solar year, the dates of Islamic holy days shift accordingly each year. In 638 A.D. the second Sunnah caliph, Umar ibn al-Khattab, dated the first year of the Islamic calendar to the year of the *Hijra* (corresponding to the Gregorian year 622 A.D.), when the Prophet Muhammad and his followers withdrew from Mecca to Medina. Each Islamic year is designated as A.H., the initials for the Latin phrase *anno Hegirae* (in the year of the *Hijra*). To roughly convert between Islamic years and Gregorian years, multiply the Islamic year by 0.97 and add 622. To convert between Gregorian years and Islamic years, subtract 622 and divide by 0.97.

For these practical reasons, as well as a general love of knowledge, scholars working at the House of Wisdom were eager to share their findings with the rest of the Muslim world. In the age before the printing press, scribes had to copy the works of Muslim scholars by hand. Scroll by elegantly lettered scroll, the works of al-Khwarizmi, Abu Kamil, and other Muslim scholars spread through the Middle East.

Some of these books found their ways to libraries attached to mosques, the Islamic places of prayer and worship. Others were sold to wealthy individuals who maintained private libraries in their homes. It is likely that Ibn al-Haytham's father was one such person. That Ibn al-Haytham received an appointment to a government office as a young man suggests that his father held a senior post in the Abbasid Caliphate. The young Ibn al-Haytham may have encountered books by Muslim scholars and translations of the works of the ancient Greeks in his father's library.

Most of Ibn al-Haytham's early education took place at the mosque of Basra. Like other mosques throughout the Muslim world, the Basran mosque served not only as a place of worship but also as a center for education. Modeled after Muhammad's original place of worship—the courtyard of his home in Medina—early mosques consisted of a large open area surrounded by columns that supported the roof. According to Muslim tradition, each teacher would take up a position by a pillar while his students sat on the floor in a semicircle around him. Dressed in flowing robes and propped against the pillar, the teacher would read from a book, deliver a lecture, or challenge the students with questions. Teachers often held their classes by the same pillar year after year. In some mosques, the names of teachers were inscribed on the pillars where they taught. Many of those names still can be seen in mosques today.

Muslim students would also be required participate in _munazarah_, or debates. As in modern debates, the participants in _munazarah_ would pose difficult and controversial questions to each other. Answers were judged on their thoroughness and soundness of logic. We know from a title of one his books, _Replies to Seven Mathematical Questions Addressed to Me in Baghdad_, that Ibn al-Haytham participated in _munazarah_ as an adult. His careful, precise writing style in this and other books reveals a nimble mind trained by the give-and-take of the _munazarah_.

Because books were difficult to reproduce in the tenth century, some teachers would order their students to write down what they said during the lectures. After several weeks or months, the students would have produced several copies of the scholar's views. The teacher would then sign each book to mark the proficiency of the student, like a modern-day diploma. Using this method of dictation, known as _tariq-i-imla_, scholars increased the chances that copies of their lectures would circulate among scholars and their ideas would spread more quickly.

The teachers in the mosques concentrated on subjects such as religion, literature, grammar, and rhetoric that today would be grouped under the heading of the humanities. The subjects known as the _ulum-al-taalim_, or the sciences—including astronomy, mathematics, medicine, and physics—were generally not taught in the mosques.

Rudolphe Ernst, an Austrian, often painted scenes from the Middle East. Painting in the European Orientalist tradition became quite popular in his lifetime. The Lesson, *an oil on canvas made in the early 1900's, portrays a teacher of the Qu'ran by his post.* (Courtesy of the Bridgeman Art Library/Private Collection.)

More often those subjects were discussed in the private homes of amateur scholars and other patrons of education.

According to an autobiographical sketch that Ibn al-Haytham wrote when he was sixty-three, he devoted much of his early education to theology, the study of the nature of God and religious truth. His theology teachers would have spent a great deal of time reading and explaining the Qur'an and the Hadith, a collection of the Prophet Muhammad's sayings. They also would have discussed how the Islamic scriptures applied to everyday practices, such as commerce, government, and law.

Although bound by tradition and the personal relationships that grew between teachers and pupils, education in Ibn al-Haytham's day was not as systematic as it is now. Students were not required to take specific courses or attend school at all. Those who wanted to study would choose a teacher and pay him a certain amount of money. Students were free to move from one teacher to another and to change their course of study at any time. After years of studying theology, this is exactly what Ibn al-Haytham did. It was a decision that would change both the direction of his life and the course of science.

TWO

Scholar of Basra

A devout Muslim, Ibn al-Haytham spent most of his life trying to know and serve his God. "I decided to discover what it is that brings us closer to God, what pleases Him most, and what makes us submissive to His ineluctable Will," he wrote in his autobiography. His restless and probing mind drove him to closely examine the doctrines of Islam. Convinced that "truth is a unitary entity" for all people, in all places, at all times, he also studied the theology of the ancient Greeks, especially Aristotle.

While still a student, Ibn al-Haytham began to examine the views held by the members of different sects, or groups, within Islam. "From my very childhood I have been reflecting on various sects and their beliefs," he wrote in his autobiography. "Each sect," he noted, "has framed its opinions and beliefs according to the principles of its faith."

The sects did not always agree about important issues. Two of the largest sects, the Shi'ah and the Sunnah, disagreed about the rightful successor of the Prophet Muhammad. The Shi'ah believed that Muhammad chose 'Ali ibn Abi Talib, his son-in-law and the father of his only surviving grandchildren, Hasan and Husayn, as his successor. The Sunnah claimed, and still claim, that the Prophet designated no successor, but encouraged his followers to choose their leader by *shura*, or consultation.

After Muhammad died, a tribe in Medina elected a local chieftain as the *khalifah* (caliph), or spiritual ruler of the Muslims. Knowing that Muhammad's followers would not accept the chieftain as caliph, some of Muhammad's kinsmen offered an alternative. They nominated Abu Bakr, the father of Muhammad's favorite wife, 'A'ishah. The leaders of the tribes agreed to this arrangement, and Abu Bakr became the first caliph. The Shi'ah, or Shi'at Ali (partisans of 'Ali), were surprised by this move, but they accepted it to keep the peace within the Muslim community. After the death of Abu Bakr and the second and third caliphs, 'Ali finally became caliph, but the reign of Muhammad's son-in-law was brief. Just five years after being named caliph, 'Ali was murdered while praying at a mosque in Kufa, Iraq.

The Sunnah then elected 'Ali's chief rival, Mu'awiyah, as the fifth caliph, and he was quickly succeeded by his son, Yazid. Mu'awiyah's progeny, known as the Umayyads, held the caliphate for over a century, although they were regarded as usurpers by the Shi'ah, who had always

The Prophet Muhammad (right) *sits with his son-in-law Ali and his grandsons Hasan and Husayn.* (Courtesy of the Granger Collection.)

believed that 'Ali was Muhammad's only rightful successor. The Shi'ah rallied behind 'Ali's son, Husayn—the grandson of the Prophet Muhammad—in the spring of

680. By then, forces loyal to Yazid viewed the Shi'ah as dangerous heretics and attacked Husayn and his followers outside the city of Karbala, Iraq. The forces loyal to Yazid soon overpowered the Shi'ah party and captured and beheaded Husayn. Shi'ah Muslims, who make up about ten percent of the world's Muslim population today, still observe the anniversary of Husayn's death as a holy day. They consider his tomb to be one of the most sacred sites in their faith.

The disagreements over the Prophet's successor led to other theological differences. Most Shi'ah believe that the twelve descendants of the Prophet, beginning with 'Ali, were special leaders known as the *imam*. According to Shi'ah theology, the *imam* were infallible and were the only ones that understood the true meaning of the Qur'an.

The Imam Husayn Shrine stands where the remains of Muhammad's grandson were buried after the Battle of Karbala. On holy days, the city of Karbala receives hundreds of thousands of pilgrims. (British Library)

After the death of the twelfth *imam*, most Shi'ah believe, other holy men, known as *mujtahids*, were given the responsibility of interpreting Islamic doctrine and law. The Sunnah, by contrast, believe that matters of doctrine can be settled by *al-jama'ah*, or "the consolidated majority." To this day, the Sunnah and Shi'ah remain divided on these and other issues.

The disagreements between the Sunnah, the Shi'ah, and other Muslim sects, such as the Sufi and Mu'tazilah, troubled young Ibn al-Haytham. He realized that if one belief was true, then a conflicting belief could not also be true; one of the beliefs must be false. False beliefs were dangerous, he reasoned, because they obscured the truth and led believers away from God. It was in the best interests of all believers, Ibn al-Haytham concluded, to identify which beliefs were true and which were false.

Although still a young man, Ibn al-Haytham took it upon himself to identify and expose false beliefs, which he likened to evil enchantments. "Having gained an insight into the intellectual bases of the sects," he wrote, "I decided to dedicate myself to the search for truth so as to tear away the veil of superstitions and doubts, which an illusive vision has cast on people, and so that the doubting and the skeptical people may lift their gaze freed from the membrane of spell and skepticism." The young theologian hoped that by revealing the truths behind the doctrines, he would be able to close the rifts that had opened between the sects.

After studying the various belief systems in depth,

Ibn al-Haytham came to a startling conclusion. He decided that the differences between the sects were rooted not in doctrine, but in the backgrounds of the various believers. "I have . . . begun to doubt the views of the various sects," he wrote, "and I am now convinced that . . . whatever differences exist between them are based not on the basic tenets of faith or the Ultimate Reality but on sociological content." This revelation brought with it a sobering realization: his study of theology had not brought him any closer to understanding the true nature of God. His disappointment was still apparent forty-five years later. "I studied in considerable detail the beliefs of various sects, thoughts, and theological systems," he wrote in his autobiography, "but I failed to gain anything which could point the way to Reality." The young scholar was frustrated. He had spent years on research that had led him nowhere. Worse, he did not know what to do next.

Ibn al-Haytham did not say how long this period of disappointment lasted, but he did explain how it came to an end: he discovered the works of the philosopher Aristotle. The words of the ancient Greek philosopher were a revelation to the young scholar. He found in Aristotle a kindred spirit and an intellectual equal, a man whose methods and insights gave him a new purpose in life. "When I discovered what Aristotle had done," he later recalled, "I became engrossed in my desire to understand philosophy wholeheartedly."

Aristotle's approach to understanding the world was broader than anything Ibn al-Haytham had encountered

ARISTOTLE

Aristotle was born in 384 B.C. in the ancient Macedonian city of Stageira. The son of a prominent doctor, Aristotle traveled to Athens at the age of eighteen to study under the great philosopher Plato at the Greek Academy. When Plato died in 344 B.C., Aristotle served for eight years as tutor to King Philip II of Macedon's son, Alexander, who later conquered most of the Middle East and Southwest Asia. After Alexander had completed his studies, Aristotle returned to Athens to begin his own school of philosophy, known as the Lyceum, where he wrote most of his important treatises. Because Aristotle liked to give his philosophical lectures while walking about, his followers were known as Peripatetics, which means "walking."

Aristotle is one of the most important figures in Western thought. He wrote on poetry, rhetoric, politics, biology, physics, astronomy, logic, and a number of other subjects. Although his conclusions on physics fell into disrepute in the sixteenth and seventeenth centuries, Aristotle laid the foundation for scientific reasoning. He believed in the value of both empirical knowledge (knowledge gleaned from the senses) and logical knowledge (knowledge deduced by the mind).

Aristotle's teacher Plato had argued that the material world is but a series of imitations of ideal forms. Inquiry, therefore, should be a top-down, strictly deductive process. Aristotle also believed in logic, and wrote even more extensively on the subject than Plato had, but thought that inquiry should begin with study of the material world, and then proceed to deduction. This was a methodology that would be employed and refined by Ibn al-Haytham. Unlike Ibn al-Haytham, however, Aristotle did not believe in experimentation. He thought that observation alone would suffice.

before. "Aristotle has discussed the nature of the physical world," he wrote. "He has analyzed causality and teleology, the celestial beings, plants and animals, Universe and Soul." What impressed Ibn al-Haytham most, however, was Aristotle's commitment to logic and reason. "He has analyzed the terminology of logic and has divided it into primary kinds," Ibn al-Haytham observed. "Furthermore, he has analyzed those aspects which are the material and elemental bases of reasoning, and he has described their classes. . . .This analysis is essential for his discussion of truth and falsehood."

Never again would Ibn al-Haytham spend his time studying matters that were unknowable and unprovable. "I saw that I can reach the truth only through concepts whose matter are sensible things, and whose form is rational," he wrote. "I found such theories present in the logic, physics, and theology of Aristotle."

Equipped with Aristotle's outlook and techniques, Ibn al-Haytham renewed his commitment to better understanding the world. "It became my belief that for gaining access to the effulgence and closeness to God, there is no better way than that of searching for truth and knowledge," he wrote. Rather than studying the words of men, he would examine the works of God. "There are three disciplines which go to make philosophy: mathematics, physical sciences, and theology," Ibn al-Haytham declared. "As long as I live, I shall keep myself pressed into the service of these disciplines."

Ibn al-Haytham could not have chosen a better place to

Islamic scholars sitting in a library discuss a book in this illustration from al-Hariri's Assemblies *written in the year 1237.* (Bibliothèque nationale de France, Paris)

embark on his journey of discovery than his own hometown of Basra. Located on the western bank of Shatt Al Arab, the waterway that connects the Tigris and Euphrates rivers with the Persian Gulf, Basra had grown from a small military outpost into a busy port city, teeming with a variety of cultures and beliefs. Merchants from Asia, Africa, and the islands of the Indian Ocean sailed to Basra to profit from its growing trade. A few of the foreign merchants decided to stay in Basra and make it their home. Small communities of Africans, Indians, Persians, and Malays flourished in the busy port city. These groups practiced their own religions and followed their own customs and traditions.

Not all of the visitors to Basra were merchants. Scholars on their way to the House of Wisdom in Baghdad often stayed as the honored guests of local patrons of learning. Sometimes the traveling scholars would be asked to lecture or to participate in a local *munazarah*. Even if Ibn al-Haytham did not participate in such discussions himself, he heard about them from others and no doubt benefited from the vibrant intellectual atmosphere of his hometown.

Ibn al-Haytham began his pursuit of philosophy by reading as many of Aristotle's works as possible. When he finished reading one of Aristotle's books, he often would write a summary of it so students and other scholars could become familiar with the philosopher's views without having to read the entire work. According to a list Ibn al-Haytham compiled at the time he wrote his autobiography, he had written at least thirteen abridgements, or summaries, of Aristotle's works by the age of sixty-three. Even so, Ibn al-Haytham did not believe his work was done. "Should God out of his limitless bounty extend my life span and grant me time to pursue my studies," he wrote, "I shall condense two books by Aristotle, one on natural healing and the other on heaven and earth."

As Ibn al-Haytham grew confident in his understanding of Aristotle's ideas, he began not only to summarize the works but also to comment on them. In one treatise Ibn al-Haytham defended Aristotle's views on the nature of the cosmos from criticism raised by a philosopher named Yahya Nahhavi. Ibn al-Haytham followed this treatise with a second, more thorough defense of Aristotle's work. He also defended one of Aristotle's books from criticism by Abu Hashim, a leader of the Mu'tazilah sect.

Ibn al-Haytham did not confine himself to the study of philosophy. He began to investigate higher mathematics and the physical sciences as well. He soon discovered that he had a gift for mathematics.

Ibn al-Haytham began his mathematical studies by reading the works of Euclid, a Greek mathematician born around 300 B.C. Euclid lived and worked in Alexandria, the ancient capital of Egypt founded by the Greek conqueror Alexander the Great in 332 B.C. Euclid's most famous book, the *Elements*, was the best introduction to geometry and number theory available in Ibn al-Haytham's day. As he did after reading Aristotle's works, Ibn al-Haytham summarized and condensed Euclid's writings. He also began analyzing them. In one book, he categorized the theorems and problems discussed by Euclid. In another, which he called "a thesaurus of mathematics," Ibn al-Haytham made discoveries of his own. "I have taken Euclid as a guide with regard to geometrical and numerical laws," he wrote of his thesaurus. "I have solved various geometrical problems and have explained the numerical problems by means of equations. I have also deviated from the postures adopted by the previous exponents of algebra."

Confident of his abilities, Ibn al-Haytham delved into the works of other ancient Greek mathematicians. He studied the works of Archimedes, a Greek mathematician and inventor who was born in 290 B.C. in Syracuse, Sicily, off the coast of Italy. In his exploration of geometry,

Archimedes grouped angles into three basic kinds. Ibn al-Haytham reflected on this idea and wrote a commentary criticizing the logic on which Archimedes had based his conclusions.

Ibn al-Haytham also studied the work of Ptolemy, an Egyptian of Greek descent who lived and worked in Alexandria around 150 A.D. In his most famous work, an astronomical manual called *Almagest*, Ptolemy used trigonometry, a branch of mathematics devoted to the study of the functions of angles, to predict the motions of the sun, moon, planets, and stars. Ibn al-Haytham was fascinated by this work and produced a summary of it, but he was not satisfied with his work. "I have not been able to derive any mathematical law of import from *Almagest*, which I have abridged and on which I have compiled a commentary," Ibn al-Haytham wrote. "If I am vouchsafed a longer life by the grace of God, I shall write another commentary which shall embody the algebraic and other mathematical disciplines thoroughly."

Ibn al-Haytham would live many more years, but his life was about to take a surprising new direction—one that threatened to keep him from writing his commentary on the *Almagest* or any other new books.

THREE

"Madness"

Just as Ibn al-Haytham began using reason and mathematics to unlock the secrets of the universe, he was appointed to a position in the government of Basra that most young men in tenth-century Iraq would have been delighted to receive. A job in the government provided a good income, a certain amount of prestige, and a lifetime of security. Ibn al-Haytham, however, feared that his duties would leave little time to study mathematics and philosophy.

The main source of information about Ibn al-Haytham's appointment to a government office comes from *Tabaqat al-Atibba*, a biographical dictionary compiled around 1250 by a Muslim historian named Ibn Abi Usaybi'ah. In addition to accounts of events in Ibn al-Haytham's life, Ibn Abi Usaybi'ah provides a copy of Ibn al-Haytham's autobiographical sketch. He also relates a story he heard from a scholar named 'Alam al-Din Qaysar ibn Abi 'l-Qasim ibn

Musafir, more commonly known as Qaysar, who was born in Upper Egypt in 1178 and died in Damascus, Syria, in 1251. According to Qaysar, Ibn al-Haytham was named a vizier, or high official, within the Muslim government.

Qaysar did not reveal why Ibn al-Haytham received this appointment. It is likely, however, that Ibn al-Haytham's family played a role in securing the post for him. Such appointments often were given to families that had proven themselves to high officials through years of loyal service. That Ibn al-Haytham received an excellent education in his youth suggests that his family was well off financially and possibly held positions in the government. Education was not free in tenth-century Iraq, and poor families could not afford to pay teachers. Ibn al-Haytham's family, by contrast, could afford for their son to study for many years. They may have supported his education because they knew that he was in line to receive a government post.

It is also possible that Ibn al-Haytham sought the appointment himself, perhaps because he had gotten married or was planning to get married and wanted to support his family. The evidence for Ibn al-Haytham's marriage comes from an inscription in the oldest surviving copy of his *Kitab al-Manazir*, or *Book of Optics*. The person who copied the manuscript gives his name as Ahmad ibn Muhammad ibn Ja'far al-'Askari. He states that he is the son-in-law of the author of the book. If Ibn al-Haytham had a son-in-law, then he must have had a daughter. If he had a daughter, then he most likely was married, since few Muslim children were born outside of wedlock in the tenth century.

Qaysar did not specify what kind of duties Ibn al-Haytham performed as vizier. Some historians believe he was a financial minister. Ibn al-Haytham later wrote a book entitled *On Business Arithmetic*, showing that he was familiar with basic financial issues. Other historians believe that Ibn al-Haytham was a civil engineer, in charge of public works projects such as the building of roads, bridges, and buildings. Ibn al-Haytham wrote several books that show a knowledge of civil engineering and surveying, including *Determination of the Altitudes of Mountains, Determination of the Height of the Pole with the Greatest Precision, On the Altitudes of Triangles*, and *On the Principles of Measurement*. Three hundred years after Ibn al-Haytham died, an Egyptian scholar still praised his *On the Principles of Measurement*. "This work is extremely useful for computing the revenue, the division of land, and the measurement of buildings," the Egyptian wrote.

Further evidence that Ibn al-Haytham may have been a civil engineer comes from another of his books, *On the Construction of the Water Clock*. This book was not about the type of clock that would sit on a desk or table, but a large piece of machinery that would be placed in a public area, often near the gate of a mosque. Ibn al-Haytham would probably not have undertaken the task of building such a large and important timepiece on his own. The scale of the project suggests that it arose from his duties as an officer of the government.

As his book about the water clock suggests, Ibn al-Haytham was fascinated by hydrodynamics, the motion of fluids. He

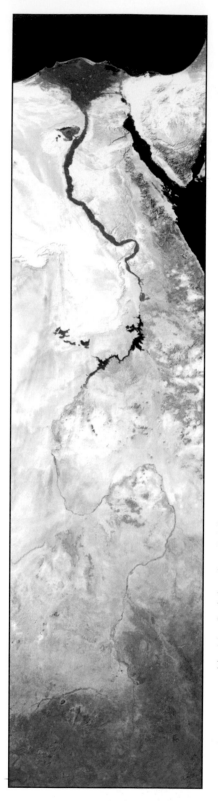

wrote at least two other books on the subject, including a work about canals and dams. He also spent some time studying the ebb and flow of the Nile River in Africa.

Rising from the shores of Lake Victoria in Uganda and flowing northward 4,132 miles to the Mediterranean Sea, the Nile is the longest river in the world. Swollen by heavy summer rains near the equator, the ancient Nile rose until it overflowed its banks in Egypt in October. The annual flooding of the Nile deposited rich, dark silt across the Egyptian floodplain, allowing farmers to cultivate the same land year after year without depleting the soil. The flood levels varied from year to year, however, causing serious problems for the Egyptian farmers. Too little flooding resulted in crop failure and famine; too much killed livestock and spread

This NASA satellite photo shows the Nile River's flow through Egypt.

disease. Once the Nile had crested, its water level dropped rapidly through the late fall and winter and continued to ebb through the spring, leaving less water for irrigation.

According to a twelfth-century historian named 'Ali ibn Zayd al-Bayhaqi, Ibn al-Haytham wrote "a book on civil engineering in which he discussed the possibility of offsetting the shortage of water in the Nile." Ibn Abi Usaybi'ah reported that Ibn al-Haytham claimed he could build a system of dams, levees, and canals that would prevent the Nile from overflowing in the fall and would preserve its waters for irrigation during the hot, dry summer. "Had I been in Egypt," Ibn al-Haytham declared, "I could have done something to regulate the Nile so that the people could derive benefit (out of its water) at its ebb and flow."

Many of the scenes along the Nile River have not changed much in the eleven centuries between Ibn al-Haytham's time and the modern day. (© Ian Sewell)

As much as these practical issues may have interested Ibn al-Haytham, they did not displace his love of pure learning. He longed to return to the study of philosophy and mathematics. His government position made this impossible, however. Qaysar reports that Ibn al-Haytham thought about resigning from his government post, but this was not realistic. He had been appointed by a high government official, probably the governor of Basra. Resigning from his post would have insulted the person who appointed him and reflected badly on his family. He could have run away, but this also would have brought dishonor to his family.

According to Qaysar, Ibn al-Haytham came up with an unusual plan to escape his duties: he pretended to be insane. At first Ibn al-Haytham's superiors were suspicious of this ruse. They relieved the young vizier of his duties, but they continued to observe him. At last convinced the illness was real, they removed him from office.

It is possible that Ibn al-Haytham was not faking his illness. In his autobiography, Ibn al-Haytham makes an intriguing statement about the inner forces that shaped his life and career. "I am not aware of the feelings, thoughts, and sensations which have guided me since my childhood," he wrote. "Call it what you may—a matter of chance, or intuition vouchsafed by Almighty God, or madness. You may attribute the source of my inspiration to any of the three." It is possible that Ibn al-Haytham claimed to be insane to set himself apart from other scholars or to make himself seem especially inspired. In his writings, however,

Ibn al-Haytham comes across as a humble person, giving credit to others and deflecting attention away from himself. It is hard to imagine that he would have tried to enhance his reputation with false claims. He took great care to avoid overstatement in his books; there is little reason to think he did otherwise in his autobiography.

A few years after being dismissed from his government appointment, Ibn al-Haytham again showed signs of mental instability. Mental illness is difficult if not impossible to cure, and recurrences are common. If Ibn al-Haytham had shown signs of mental illness only once, he might well have been faking his symptoms. That he experienced a relapse suggests his problems were real.

From what is known about his personality and beliefs, it also would have been out of character for Ibn al-Haytham to mislead government officials. He often said that pursuing the truth was most important thing in life. Deceiving the government about his mental fitness would have been no small breech of truth; it would have been an elaborate hoax that would have to have spanned months, if not years. It would have required not just one lie, but an endless stream of them. Such a deception would have affected not only Ibn al-Haytham, but also many people close to him, including his family, friends, and associates. He would have had to have fooled them all, or else let them in on his secret, making them accomplices in his scheme to defraud the government and putting them at risk of punishment.

This behavior seems incongruous with what is known of Ibn al-Haytham's character and his commitment to Islam, which condemns lying. On the other hand, his writings show no signs of mental instability. Furthermore, it is possible that his passion for pure learning was so intense that it drove him to perpetrate his scheme.

Real or fake, Ibn al-Haytham's mental breakdown allowed him to escape the drudgery of his government job. His freedom restored, he returned to the pursuits he loved—mathematics, geometry, and philosophy. At last, it seemed, he would be able to write his commentary on the *Almagest*.

Once again, however, Ibn al-Haytham's life took an unexpected turn. One day around 1010, a stranger showed up at Ibn al-Haytham's door. The visitor bore a message from Al-Hakim Bi-amr Allah, the sixth ruler of the Fatimid dynasty of Egypt. Al-Hakim had learned of Ibn al-Haytham's statements about taming the Nile. The Egyptian leader wanted to discuss the Iraqi scholar's plan in person. Ibn al-Haytham was to come to Egypt immediately.

FOUR

To Egypt

None of the twelfth-century historians who told of Ibn al-Haytham's summons to Egypt described how he felt about the invitation to meet with al-Hakim. On one hand, al-Hakim was a wealthy and powerful leader who prized learning. He patronized scholars such as astronomer Ibn Yunus and built the Dar al-'Ilm library in Cairo, which rivaled the House of Wisdom in Baghdad. He built several mosques and was considered a holy man. The Isma'ili sect of Shi'ah Muslims believed that al-Hakim, whose full name, Al-Hakim Bi-amr Allah, means "Ruler by God's Command" in Arabic, was a descendant of the Prophet Muhammad. Since Ibn al-Haytham had voiced his desire to control the flooding of the Nile, he no doubt felt honored to be approached by such an important figure. If he succeeded in taming the Nile, al-Hakim would probably reward him generously.

Al-Hakim, who became Caliph at eleven years old, was so erratic that Egyptian law changed to prevent a minor from absolute rule. As an adult, however, he finished building this mosque started by his father. The Al-Hakim Mosque, completed in 1013, is the second-largest Fatimid mosque in Cairo. (Library of Congress)

On the other hand, al-Hakim was known as a strange and capricious leader. For example, he once ordered the slaughter of all dogs in Cairo because their barking annoyed him. He could be cruel to human beings as well. Shortly after coming to power, he ordered the destruction of the city of al-Fustat, near Cairo, the capital of the Fatimid dynasty. Throughout his reign, he persecuted Sunnah Muslims, Jews, and Christians. For these and other reasons, al-Hakim was called "The Mad Caliph." Even if Ibn al-Haytham was pleased with the prospect of putting his ideas into action, he probably had misgivings about serving such a violent and unpredictable leader.

ORIGINS OF THE FATIMID DYNASTY

Al-Hakim Bi-amr Allah (The Mad Caliph) ruled over the Fatimid dynasty, which extended over most of North Africa from 910 to 1171. The word Fatimid is derived from "Fatima," who was the Prophet Muhammad's daughter and the husband of 'Ali ibn Abi Talib, the man Shi'ah Muslims consider to be the rightful successor to Muhammad. The Fatimids belonged to a Shi'ah sect named the Isma'ili.

All Shi'ah believe that the succession of the caliphate should pass through the descendants of Fatima and 'Ali, but an issue arose after the death of Ja'far al-Sadiq, the sixth Shi'ah Imam. Both of al-Sadiq's two sons, Musa al-Kazim and Isma'il bin Jafar, had claims to become the seventh Imam. Most Shi'ah supported Musa and his progeny, up through the twelfth Imam; they are thus known as Twelvers and today constitute about eighty percent of all Shi'ah. Isma'il's supporters were known as Isma'ilis, or Seveners, because they believed Isma'il was the last (and seventh) rightful Imam. The Isma'ili were a small but dedicated group that established power in Yemen and eventually sent emissaries to conquer North Africa.

The first Fatimid caliph, Ubayd Allah al-Mahdi Billah, assumed power in 909. He claimed to be descended from Fatima and 'Ali, through Isma'il, although many Muslim theologians, both then and now, disputed this claim. The Fatimids were the first power in the Middle East to seriously challenge the power of the Sunnah Abbasid Caliphate in two hundred years. They built up a flourishing trade empire that included ports on both the Mediterranean and Red Seas. In 970, when Ibn al-Haytham was just five years old, they conquered Egypt and relocated the capital to Cairo. Caliph al-Hakim was Ubayd's great-great-great grandson.

Ibn al-Haytham must have had concerns about giving up the study of philosophy and mathematics once again. He knew that building a dam on the Nile would take years, if not an entire lifetime. If he accepted this monumental task, he might have to put off his studies indefinitely. Ibn al-Haytham had resented his duties in the government of Basra. His duties in Egypt would be even more demanding.

Even if Ibn al-Haytham had second thoughts about going to Egypt, there was not much he could do about it. Declining such an offer would have insulted one of the most powerful and dangerous men in the Muslim world. Al-Hakim easily could have responded to such a refusal with violence or other punishment. The Egyptian ruler certainly had the means to enforce his wishes, even in faraway Iraq.

Pleased with the invitation or not, Ibn al-Haytham left for Egypt late in 1010 or early in 1011. He probably traveled north along the Tigris River to Baghdad, west to Damascus, south through Jerusalem, west across the Sinai Peninsula, and finally into Egypt—a total distance of 950 miles. His journey would have taken between two and four months, depending on whether he traveled by foot, donkey, or camel. If he stopped in various cities along the way—to visit the House of Wisdom in Baghdad, for example—the journey would have taken even longer. Two medieval historians, ‘Ali ibn Zayd al-Bayhaqi and Jamal al-Din ibn al-Qifti, described what happened when Ibn al-Haytham arrived in Egypt. The two accounts differ, but both agree that Ibn al-Haytham met al-Hakim face-to-face.

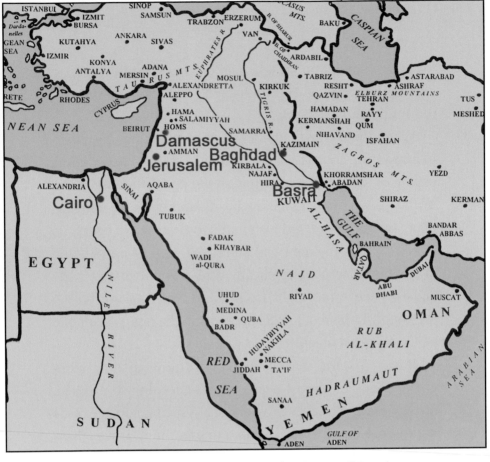

Ibn al-Haytham's probable route from Basra to Cairo.

The earliest account comes from 'Ali ibn Zayd al-Bayhaqi, a historian who died about thirty years after Ibn al-Haytham did. According to al-Bayhaqi, when Ibn al-Haytham arrived in Cairo he made his way to an inn. After resting for a few days, he received word that al-Hakim was outside the gate of the inn, asking for him. When Ibn al-Haytham reached the street, he found the caliph seated on a donkey that wore a silver-plated harness. A short man, Ibn al-Haytham climbed up on a bench to speak with the caliph eye-to-eye. He presented the Egyptian leader with his treatise about building a dam on the Nile and began to explain his plan. Al-Hakim listened as he looked through the Iraqi scholar's book.

When Ibn al-Haytham had finished speaking, the caliph glanced up. "You are wrong," said al-Hakim, "because the expenses likely to be incurred on the project are in excess of the gains." To emphasize his disappointment with the plan, al-Hakim ordered his guards to destroy the bench on which Ibn al-Haytham had stood. "At this, Abu Ali [Ibn al-Haytham] was overcome by dire fear for his own life and fled the same night from Cairo," al-Bayhaqi wrote. "At long last he reached Syria and sought refuge with one of the Syrian nobles."

Jamal al-Din ibn al-Qifti's account differs from al-Bayhaqi's in almost every way. According to al-Qifti, al-Hakim was so eager to meet Ibn al-Haytham that he rode out to the village of al-Khandaq to greet him. It was there that Ibn al-Haytham described his scheme for controlling the Nile. In al-Qifti's account, al-Hakim did not ridicule the plan. On the contrary, the Egyptian leader was so impressed by Ibn al-Haytham and his ideas that he pledged to give the Iraqi scholar all of the workers and money he would need to complete the project.

With al-Hakim's backing, Ibn al-Haytham traveled six hundred miles south along the Nile to the village of al-Janadil, near Aswan, where he proposed to build his dam. Along the way, Ibn al-Haytham's party passed the pyramids of the ancient Egyptian pharaohs. Ibn al-Haytham was impressed by the precision and scale of these huge monuments. He had never seen anything like them, and he began to wonder about the engineers who built them. If they had been capable of creating these massive tombs, he reasoned, then they must have been capable of building a dam on the Nile. That they did not do so concerned him.

Once Ibn al-Haytham reached al-Janadil, he saw that he was right in thinking it was an ideal place to build a dam. Granite banks rise from each side of the river, forming a natural channel. Ibn al-Haytham realized that if workers could block the north end of the channel with a stone dam, the water would not be able to flow around it. Held in by the granite banks, the water would rise behind the dam, forming a lake.

The problems arose when Ibn al-Haytham measured the opening between the banks. The river itself is 1,800 feet wide, but the opening in the granite is more than 3,200 feet wide at ground level—four times wider than the base of the Great Pyramid of Khufu. The banks do not rise straight up from ground level, but instead slope away from the river. At a point 360 feet above the river, the banks stand more than 12,000 feet apart—sixteen times the width of the Great Pyramid. Ibn al-Haytham realized that the scope of the project exceeded the resources at his command. Nine hundred years after Ibn al-Haytham surveyed the site, the Egyptian government built a dam across the Nile on the very spot Ibn al-Haytham proposed. The twentieth-century builders used nearly 58 million cubic yards of material to construct the Aswan High Dam, roughly seventeen times the amount of material ancient builders used to build the Great Pyramid.

Considering al-Hakim's reputation as a violent and unstable man, Ibn al-Haytham probably had doubts about telling him the bad news. Under the circumstances, it would not have been surprising if Ibn al-Haytham had fled from Egypt, fearing for his life, as al-Bayhaqi suggested he did. According to al-Qifti, however, Ibn al-Haytham traveled to Cairo, met with al-Hakim, and admitted that his plan would not work.

Al-Hakim did not react to Ibn al-Haytham's report as a Mad Caliph might have been expected to. On the contrary, al-Hakim took the news calmly. Rather than punishing Ibn al-Haytham for his failure, al-Hakim offered him a position in his government. According to al-Qifti, Ibn al-Haytham accepted the post "out of fear, not desire."

Not long after accepting the appointment, Ibn al-Haytham began to have second thoughts about serving al-Hakim. Al-Qifti suggests that Ibn al-Haytham worried that al-Hakim would have a change of heart and order his punishment, perhaps even his execution. Ibn al-Haytham also may have viewed this government job in the same way that he viewed his job in Basra—as an impediment to his own research. Whatever the reason, Ibn al-Haytham sought a way out of his new post. According to al-Qifti, he employed the same ruse he had used in Basra, once again pretending to be mad.

It is worth noting that while al-Qifti and al-Bayhaqi both reported that Ibn al-Haytham escaped a government post by pretending to be insane, they did not agree on where this happened. Al-Bayhaqi says it occurred in Basra; al-Qifti says it occurred in Egypt. Neither historian says it happened twice. Since al-Bayhaqi died one hundred years before al-Qifti did, al-Qifti may have borrowed the insanity story from him and transferred it to Egypt. It is also possible, however, that both accounts are true. Ibn al-Haytham may have pretended to be insane in Egypt precisely because the ruse had worked so well in Basra.

It is also possible that neither episode was staged. Nothing that is known about Ibn al-Haytham's character suggests that he would be willing to carry out such an elaborate hoax once, let alone twice. It certainly would have been more difficult to do so in Cairo than in Basra. Al-Hakim was a bright man, and he surrounded himself with intelligent advisors. Ibn al-Haytham's ruse would have to be extremely convincing to fool the Egyptian leader's court. It also would have been much more dangerous to attempt the hoax in Egypt than it would have been in Basra. Al-Hakim's violent history suggests he would not have hesitated to severely punish or even execute anyone who tried to fool him.

Whatever its cause, Ibn al-Haytham's breakdown did not work with al-Hakim as it had with the officials in Basra. Al-Hakim placed the Iraqi scholar under house arrest, confining him to a single house or room within Cairo. The Mad Caliph also took away Ibn al-Haytham's possessions. Al-Qifti's account does not specify how al-Hakim enforced Ibn al-Haytham's confinement. Presumably he stationed guards outside the residence and had servants take food to the prisoner.

Days faded into weeks, weeks in months, and months into years as Ibn al-Haytham remained confined to a dwelling in Cairo. Stripped of his possessions, he could neither read nor write. Yet his mind was not necessarily dormant. Prisoners have been known to do amazing things to keep their minds occupied. Some have composed poems and even entire books and committed them to memory. Others have scratched writings and drawings into the walls of their cells. Given how active Ibn al-Haytham's mind was, it seems unlikely that he did nothing during the years that he was held under house arrest. In fact, his confinement may have led to the greatest breakthrough of his career.

FIVE

Scholar of Cairo

The first device used for projecting an image onto a flat surface was known in Europe as the camera obscura. This term was derived from two Latin words: *camera,* meaning room or chamber, and *obscura,* meaning darkened. The original camera obscura was just that—a darkened room with a small opening, or aperture, that allowed light to shine onto a wall or screen. The light on the surface formed a color image—upside down and backwards—of whatever was outside the room, across from the aperture. Although the term *camera obscura* is Latin, the invention is not. It was described in *Kitab al-Manazir,* or *The Book of Optics,* by Ibn al-Haytham.

The Book of Optics is Ibn al-Haytham's most important work. In it the Iraqi scholar corrected misconceptions about vision and light that scholars had believed for centuries. For example, many of the ancient Greeks believed that human beings were able to see because the eyes sent out rays that sensed objects. Ibn al-Haytham showed that the opposite was true: vision occurs when rays of light enter the eye and stimulate the optic nerve. It was the first time in history that a person had accurately described the mechanics of sight. Ibn al-Haytham did not stop there, however. Building on the work of earlier scholars such as Aristotle, Euclid, Ptolemy, Theon of Alexandria, and Ya'qub ibn Ishaq as-Sabah al-Kindi, Ibn al-Haytham created a unified theory of light, correctly describing its propagation, reflection, and refraction. _The Book of Optics_ remained the leading source of knowledge about optics for the next five hundred years.

The most important thing about _The Book of Optics_ is not the discoveries it contains but the way in which Ibn al-Haytham arrived at and supported those discoveries. He was the first person to systematically construct devices—such as the camera obscura—to test hypotheses and verify the accuracy of his findings. By using concrete, physical experiments to support his conclusions, Ibn al-Haytham helped establish the modern scientific method.

The Book of Optics was not Ibn al-Haytham's first book about vision. In the introduction to _The Book of Optics_, Ibn al-Haytham states that he wrote a treatise on optics earlier in his career. This work was probably a commentary on another book, such as Ptolemy's _Optics_. Ibn al-Haytham admits that he "followed persuasive methods of reasoning" in his earlier work, but he did not verify his findings with what he called "true demonstrations." The lack of experimental proof in the first book was such a great flaw, Ibn al-Haytham wrote that anyone who finds the work should disregard it.

At some point, Ibn al-Haytham came up with a new way to test and prove the facts about optics. How did this breakthrough occur? One clue emerges from the text of *The Book of Optics*: it is a very solitary book. In it Ibn al-Haytham describes dozens of experiments, but only one—an experiment using a wooden block drilled with two holes to let light into a room—calls for the use of

A leaf from Al-Haytham's The Book of Optics, *complete with illustrating diagram.* (Staatsbibliothek zu Berlin)

an assistant. The rest of the experiments are designed to be carried out by one person. The objects used in the experiments are few and simple: bare walls, stopped-up windows, screens, lamps, and tubes. The entire work has the feeling of having been composed in an empty room. Perhaps it was. It is possible that the world's first camera obscura was a prison cell in Cairo.

Ibn al-Haytham left no record of what he did for the years that al-Qifti says he was under house arrest. If, as al-Qifti says, al-Hakim took away Ibn al-Haytham's possessions, the Iraqi scholar would not have had any of the books he brought to Egypt. As a result, he would not have been able to write his long-deferred commentary on the *Almagest* or commentaries on any other books. If he was not allowed to go outside, he would not have been able to observe enough of the night sky to write about astronomy. He would, however, have been able to watch the sky lighten at dawn, observe shafts of sunlight cut through his room in the afternoon, and ponder the light given off by an oil lamp in the evening. It is possible that Ibn al-Haytham realized how to conduct "true demonstrations relating to all objects of vision," as he describes his task in *The Book of Optics*, during his long imprisonment. If his guards allowed him to have writing materials, he may have written some or all of *The Book of Optics* during his confinement in Cairo.

Ibn al-Haytham begins *The Book of Optics* by discussing the two theories of vision that had been circulating since the time of the ancient Greeks. The first theory—advanced

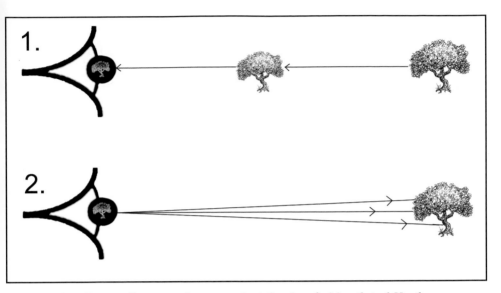

This diagram illustrates the two ancient theories of vision that al-Haytham disagreed with in his The Book of Optics.

by Aristotle and his followers, whom Ibn al-Haytham calls "the physicists"—states that "vision is effected by a form which comes from the visible object to the eye." The second theory—primarily advanced by Ptolemy and Euclid, whom Ibn al-Haytham calls "the mathematicians"—states that "vision is effected by a ray which issues from the eye to the visible object." "These two notions," Ibn al-Haytham wrote, "appear to diverge and contradict one another if taken at face value." He continues:

> Now, for any two different doctrines, it is either the case that one of them is true and the other false; or they are both false, the truth being other than either of them; or they both lead to one thing which is the truth. . . .That being the case . . . and because the

manner of vision has not been ascertained, we have thought it appropriate that we direct our attention to this subject as much as we can, and seriously apply ourselves to it, and examine it, and diligently inquire into its nature.

Perhaps because he began work on _The Book of Optics_ while in prison, stripped of all his books and possessions, Ibn al-Haytham rarely cites earlier authorities in the book. Instead, he relies on his own observations, demonstrations, and analyses. His approach, he says, will be systematic:

We should distinguish the properties of particulars, and gather by induction what pertains to the eye when vision takes place and what is found in the manner of sensation to be uniform, unchanging, manifest, and not subject to doubt. After which we should ascend in our inquiry and reasonings, gradually and orderly, criticizing premises and exercising caution in regard to conclusions—our aim in all that we make subject to inspection and review being to employ justice, not to follow prejudice, and to take care in all that we judge and criticize that we seek the truth and not be swayed by opinion.

To eliminate opinion and prejudice, Ibn al-Haytham supports his assertions with experimental or mathematical proofs whenever possible. Just five paragraphs after the introduction, for example, Ibn al-Haytham states that straight lines exist between "the surface of the eye" and "each point on the seen surface of the object." He continues,

"An accurate experimental examination of this fact may be easily made with the help of rulers and tubes."

He then describes how an observer looking through a straight tube will see only the part of an object that lies directly across from the opening of the tube. "If . . . he covers any part of the opening, then there will be screened off only that portion that lies on a straight line with the eye and the screening body—this straightness being secured by the ruler and the straightness of the tube," he writes. "It follows from this experiment, with a necessity that dispels doubt, that sight does not perceive any visible object existing with it in the same atmosphere, the perception being not by reflection, except through straight lines alone that can be imagined to extend between the surface of the object and the surface of the eye."

The most important discovery in *The Book of Optics* appears in the very next sentence: "Sight does not perceive any visible object unless there exists in the object some light, which the object possesses of itself or which radiates upon it from another object." With this simple observation, Ibn al-Haytham solved the mystery of vision that had baffled scholars for centuries. It was light, not the physical "forms" described by the physicists, that traveled from visible objects to the eye. The rays that create vision do not travel out of the eye, as the mathematicians said, but into it. Those rays are light rays.

Although Ibn al-Haytham had set out to write a book about vision, he soon realized that vision and light were inextricably linked. Consequently, a significant portion of

The Book of Optics is devoted to the study of light. Ibn al-Haytham begins by dividing light into two basic groups: primary light and secondary light. Primary light is the light radiated by an illuminating body, such as a lamp, a fire, the stars, or the sun. Secondary light is primary light that has been reflected off another surface. During the day, for example, the sun provides primary light, while every other visible object—a bird, a tree, a stone, a blade of grass—reflects the light of the sun. Even the atmosphere reflects light, Ibn al-Haytham wrote, which is why the sky brightens even before the sun rises.

All light—both primary and secondary—travels in rays, originating at a single point and moving in a straight line away from that point. The light of the sun, for example,

Primary light falls from the sun to illuminate a tree branch. The secondary light then bounces off in all directions, including the direction of an observing eye.

travels from a point on the sun's surface in a straight line through space. If a ray of sunlight strikes an opaque object on earth, that object will reflect it. The light reflected by an opaque object also forms a ray. It originates from a point on the surface of the object and travels away from it in a straight line.

Ibn al-Haytham points out that light radiates in all directions from its source. "The light shining from a self-luminous body into the transparent air," he writes, "radiates from every part of the luminous body facing that air . . . and it issues from every point on the luminous body in every straight line that can be imagined to extend in the air from that point."

To prove that light radiates from every point of a luminous object—not just the center, the ends, or the whole—Ibn al-Haytham describes an experiment similar to the one he used to prove that visual rays travel in straight lines. He starts with a sheet of copper with a large, circular hole in the center. Through this hole, he proposes that the experimenter slide "a well-straightened cylindrical tube of regular circularity and convenient length." One end of the tube is open. The other end is closed, but punctured by an aperture, which should "not exceed the thickness of a needle." The experimenter then holds a candle up to the open end of the cylinder "in the darkness of night" and holds an opaque object up to the aperture at the other end. Only a small amount of the light from the flame passes through the aperture. The rest of the light is blocked by the sheet of copper.

Then, he suggests, "the experimenter should . . . gently move the flame so another part of it may face the hole, and then inspect the body opposite." As the flames moves, the light projected onto the opaque object changes: when the tip of the flame is opposite the aperture, the light on the object is narrow and dim; but when the center of the flame is opposite the aperture, the light on the object is wide and bright. "Therefore," he concludes, "it appears from this experiment that light radiates from each part of the fire."

What is true of primary light is also true of secondary light. "From the light that shines on any body, light radiates in every opposite direction," Ibn al-Haytham writes. This was an especially important discovery because it explains why vision remains steady even when the viewer's eye moves. According to Ibn al-Haytham's theory, a single point on any object radiates light rays into the air in all directions. If one of the rays enters the eye, it enables the viewer to see that point on the object. That same point also sends out countless rays of light that do not enter the eye. If the viewer moves his or her head slightly, the ray that originally entered the eye will miss it, but another ray, originating from the same point, will enter it. Since there are an infinite number of rays radiating from a single point, they will continue to stream into the eye as the viewer moves, providing the viewer with an uninterrupted view of that point.

Ibn al-Haytham was not content to simply assert that reflected light radiates in all directions; he was determined to prove it. To do so, he devised an ingenious demonstration involving darkened rooms and the light of dawn. He starts with a rectangular building with outer walls that face north, south, east, and west. The eastern wall, he writes, should have "an opening or door at the top of the wall" that allows sunlight to enter the room, striking the western wall. Directly across from the western wall is the opening to a darkened chamber. "The experimenter should observe the place when morning light shines on that wall through the opening opposite, which should be fairly wide. He will find the chamber illuminated by that light, and the light in the chamber weaker than the light on that wall. Then, as the light on the wall grows stronger, so will the light in the chamber." In other words, the darkened chamber is being lit indirectly, by light reflected by the sunlit wall.

Ibn al-Haytham then proposes a second chamber positioned inside the first chamber. He finds that it, too, is illuminated. The only light entering the building comes through the opening in the eastern wall. This light illuminates the western wall, which reflects light in all directions, illuminating not only the eastern wall, but also the floor, the ceiling, and all parts of the room, including the back wall of the darkened chamber. Every illuminated point in the room, in turn, sends out light rays in all directions, so that light enters not only the darkened chamber, but also the second chamber within it. The light grows weaker each time it is reflected, but it still reaches the inner chamber.

One of Ibn al-Haytham's most important achievements was to investigate the implications of his own findings. In

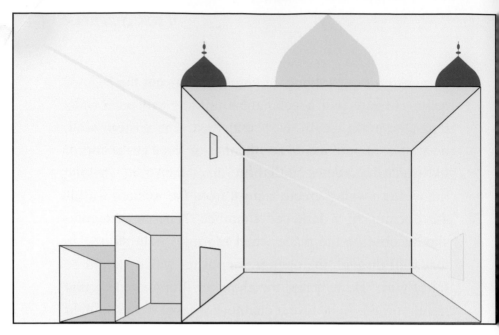

This diagram illustrates Ibn al-Haytham's experiment that proved light radiates in all directions.

doing so, he helped to develop what would later become known as the hypothetico-deductive method of inquiry. This method states that a possible explanation, or hypothesis, cannot be fully proven unless the consequences that follow from it are also proven to be true.

Ibn al-Haytham's theory of vision suggested that light rays emanate in all directions from all illuminated objects. If this really is the case, Ibn al-Haytham deduced, each light ray must intersect, or cross, many other light rays. If intersecting light rays have any effect on each other, he reasoned, "it follows that these colours and lights will be mixed in the atmosphere and in the transparent bodies and will have reached the eye mixed; and they will affect the body of the eye while they are mixed, and thus neither the colours of the visible objects nor the objects [themselves] will be distinguished by the eye." Everyday experience suggests that this does not happen. The eye can view several objects at the same time with complete clarity. Therefore, Ibn al-Haytham concluded, light rays must be able to intersect with each other without interference. Ibn al-Haytham understood that he had to prove this, or else his entire theory would be in doubt. To prove that light rays intersect without affecting each other, he designed what would become the most famous experiment in *The Book of Optics*.

Ibn al-Haytham proposes that the experimenter position several lamps at various points in the same area, "all being opposite a single aperture leading to a dark place." On the other side of the aperture is a blank wall where the experimenter can observe the effects of the light passing through the aperture. He finds that the various lights pass through the aperture along straight paths and appear separately on the blank wall. "If one of the lamps is screened," Ibn al-Haytham observes, "only the light opposite that lamp in the dark will vanish. When the screen is moved away from the lamp, that light will return to its place. Whichever lamp is screened, only the light facing it in the [dark] place will disappear. When the screen is removed, the light will return to its place."

Ibn al-Haytham then proposes a variation on the same experiment, this one employing more lamps and "a chamber with a two-panel door in the dark night," which yields the same results as his original experiment. His results confirmed, Ibn al-Haytham reasons that "all the lights that appear in the dark place have reached it through the aperture alone . . . therefore the lights of all those lamps have come together at the aperture, then separated after passing through it. Thus, if lights blended in the atmosphere, the lights of the lamps meeting at the aperture would have mixed in the air at the aperture . . . and they would have come out so mingled together that they would not be subsequently distinguishable. We do not, however, find the matter to be so; rather the lights are found to come out separately, each being opposite the lamp from which it has arrived."

This experiment embodies all of the elements of Ibn al-Haytham's method of inquiry. He begins by stating the problem or question: do lights rays affect each other when they intersect? Next, he gathers information by observing how light behaves in various circumstances. Based on these observations, he offers a possible answer, or hypothesis: lights rays are able to intersect without being affected by each other. He then constructs a simple experiment to test this hypothesis, forcing the lights from different lamps to cross at a single point. After repeating his experiment and confirming his results, he finds that the evidence supports his hypothesis. This systematic, step-by-step approach, based on both sound logic and observed fact, would come to be known as the scientific method. It is the method of inquiry that scientists around the world continue to use, in various incarnations, to this day.

Ibn al-Haytham's lamp experiment also would gain fame because it offered the first full description of what would later become known as a camera obscura. Other scholars such as Aristotle, Theon of Alexandria, and al-Kindi had all previously described ways to project an image using an aperture. As a result, each has been credited with creating a kind of camera obscura. For example, Aristotle noted that sunlight traveling through small openings between the leaves of a tree, the holes of a sieve, the openings of wickerwork, and even interlaced fingers will create circular patches of light on the ground. He also noted that during a solar eclipse, these patches of light—which are actually images of the sun—will change shape. He even built a box with a small hole to let in sunlight to better observe this phenomenon.

Theon of Alexandria, a fourth-century mathematician, also experimented with small apertures, or pinholes. He observed how candlelight passing through a pinhole will create an illuminated spot on a screen that is directly in line with the aperture and the center of the candle. From this observation, which he described in his book *The Recension of the* Optics *of Euclid*, Theon deduced that light rays travel in straight lines. Five centuries later, al-Kindi, a ninth-century Muslim philosopher, repeated Theon's candle experiment. Al-Kindi noted that not only does the light from the center of the candle's flame proceed in a straight line, but the light from each edge of the flame also proceeds in a straight line. Using a diagram, al-Kindi showed that light from the right side of the flame will pass through the aperture and end up on the left side of the screen, while light from the left side of the flame will pass through the aperture and end up on the right side of the screen.

Ibn al-Haytham knew of at least some of these

experiments and no doubt was influenced by them. His lamp experiment expanded on the earlier experiments in important ways, however. For one thing, each of the earlier experiments involved only one source of light—the sun or a single candle flame. While Aristotle, Theon, and al-Kindi accurately described the effects of a single light passing through a pinhole, none of them suggested that what is being projected onto the screen is an image of everything on the other side of the aperture. By arranging several different light sources across a large area, Ibn al-Haytham leaves little doubt that an image is being projected onto the screen, even if it is only an image of lights. In the second version of his experiment, where he talks about arranging lamps outside a door, Ibn al-Haytham can be said to be describing the first camera obscura because he is projecting an image from outdoors onto a screen indoors.

Ibn al-Haytham's lamp experiment shows that light from several sources, when projected through a small hole, will not merge but will appear separately on the other side.

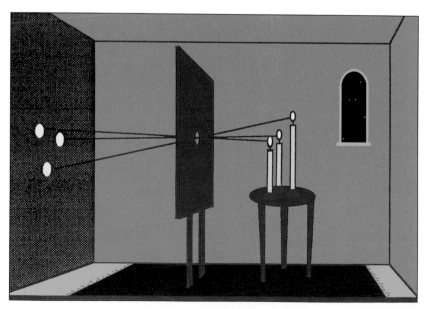

As important as Ibn al-Haytham's experiments with light would prove to be, they make up only small portion of *The Book of Optics*. Ibn al-Haytham divided his massive work into seven sections, or books. His experiments with lamps come from Book I, which is devoted to "the manner of vision generally." In addition to descriptions of the properties of light, Book I also contains a chapter on "the structure of the eye." Drawing on the work of Galen and other medical scholars, Ibn al-Haytham describes the parts of the eye in precise, even graphic detail. He correctly explains how the cornea refracts, or bends, light rays as they enter the eye. He also suggests that the optic nerve carries visual sensations to the brain.

Ibn al-Haytham was the first scientist to maintain that vision occurs in the brain, not in the eyes. By doing so, he pioneered what has become known as the psychology of visual perception. He argued that personal experience affects how and what people see. For example, a small child with little experience may have a hard time interpreting things he or she sees. At the same time, an adult can make mistakes in vision because experience suggests that he or she is seeing one thing, when really he or she is seeing another. Ibn al-Haytham was so fascinated by errors of vision that he devoted all of Book III to the topic. Perhaps it was this awareness—that vision and perception are more subjective than most people allow—that confirmed Ibn al-Haytham's faith in a rigorous, skeptical approach to scientific inquiry.

Like other scholars, such as Archimedes and Ptolemy, Ibn al-Haytham was fascinated by the effects that flat and

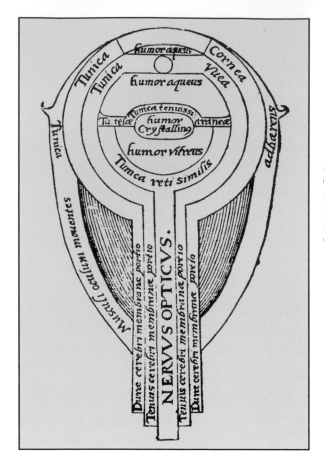

Al-Haytham's understanding of the eye, as illustrated in Risner's 1572 Opticae thesaurus—*which included a Latin translation of* The Book of Optics.

curved mirrors have on light. He devoted Book IV to "reflection from smooth bodies," Book V to "the forms seen inside smooth bodies," and Book VI to "errors in sight in what it perceives by reflection." He also was interested in the way that transparent objects, such as water and glass, refract light. He devoted Book VII to "the manner of visual perception by refraction through transparent bodies." In all four of these books, Ibn al-Haytham uses high-level geometry and mathematics to explain the behavior of light.

Book V contains one of the most enduring problems posed by ancient mathematics. Ibn al-Haytham imagined a scenario involving an observer, a light source, and a spherical mirror, all three in fixed locations. The observer looks upon the spherical mirror, which reflects the light from the light source. Ibn al-Haytham tried to determine the point on the spherical mirror where the light is reflected to the eye of the observer. The question had originally been formulated by Ptolemy in 150 A.D., but because Ibn al-Haytham considered it so extensively, it is known as "Alhazen's Problem" in the West. Ibn al-Haytham solved the problem using a geometric proof, but an algebraic solution to the problem eluded mathematicians until the end of the twentieth century.

Despite its brilliance, *The Book of Optics* is not free from errors. Many of Ibn al-Haytham's findings were later proven wrong. Perhaps his greatest error was his failure to understand that the eye works like a small camera obscura, with the pupil acting as an aperture that projects a small image—upside down and backwards—onto the part of the eye known as the retina. This discovery would not be made for another six hundred years, when a German scientist named Johannes Kepler accurately described how an image forms within the eye. Kepler and other scientists who proved portions of *The Book of Optics* wrong all did so by using the scientific method.

SIX

Return to Basra

For ten long years Ibn al-Haytham remained under house arrest in Cairo. Whether he spent this time recovering from mental illness, inventing "true demonstrations relating to all objects of vision," or simply languishing in his cell is not known for certain. What is known is that on the night of February 13, 1021, Ibn al-Haytham's captor, Caliph Al-Hakim Bi-amr Allah, went for a walk in the Muqattam Hills and never returned. The Mad Caliph simply vanished. According to Ibn al-Qifti, government officials informed Ibn al-Haytham of this development, restored his possessions to him, and released him.

For the first time in ten years, Ibn al-Haytham was free to go anywhere he pleased. After years of incarceration, however, he had no money and no place to stay. Ibn

Azhar mosque was built in 972 and named after the Prophet's daughter Fatima al-Zahraa, through whom the Fatimid Caliphs trace their lineage. When the first lecture was held in 975, Azhar mosque became the site of the oldest university in the world. Today, the school is a prestigious center of Islamic learning. (Library of Congress)

al-Qifti reports that Ibn al-Haytham made his way to the Azhar mosque in Cairo, where clerical leaders allowed him to take up residence in a domed room or tent by the gate of the mosque.

According to the twelfth-century Jewish philosopher and physician Joseph ben Judah, who lived in Cairo around 1185, Ibn al-Haytham supported himself by copying manuscripts. Joseph ben Judah told Ibn al-Qifti that he had heard that Ibn al-Haytham charged "the non-negotiable price" of 150 Egyptian dinars for making one copy each of Euclid's *Elements*, Ptolemy's *Almagest*, and the so-called *Intermediate Books*, a collection of works on astronomy and mathematics that included Euclid's *Data*, *Optics*, and

This copy of Ptolemy's Almagest, produced in the fourteenth century, features animals with stargazing tools and a woman teaching an astronomy lesson. The woman, Astronomy personified, leads a student by the hand. (British Library)

Phenomena. Ibn al-Haytham lived on the sale of one set of these books each year, according to Joseph ben Judah. He may have copied other books as well. The Ayasofya Library in Istanbul, Turkey, has in its collection an Arabic translation of Apollonius's *Conics* that was copied and signed by Ibn al-Haytham.

Ibn al-Haytham also appears to have been a teacher while in Cairo. Ibn Abi Usaybi'ah reports that an Egyptian scholar named al-Mubashshir ibn Fatik studied mathematics and astronomy with Ibn al-Haytham. Usaybi'ah also claims that a philosopher named Ishaq ibn Yunus studied algebra with the Iraqi polymath.

Ali ibn Zayd al-Bayhaqi tells an unusual story about Ibn al-Haytham's attitude toward learning. According to al-Bayhaqi, a Syrian nobleman named Surkhab came to Ibn al-Haytham and asked if he could study with him. Ibn al-Haytham agreed to tutor the nobleman but demanded one hundred dinars a month for payment. The price was high, but Surkhab did not hesitate to pay the fee. For three years the Syrian studied with Ibn al-Haytham. At the end of this time, his education complete, Surkhab bid his tutor farewell. Ibn al-Haytham asked the nobleman to wait a moment. "You deserve this money all the more," Ibn al-Haytham said, returning all 3,600 dinars to Surkhab, "since I just wished to test your sincerity and, when I saw that for the sake of learning you cared little for money, I devoted full attention towards your education. Do remember that, in any righteous cause, it is not good to accept a return, a bribe, or a gift."

Ibn al-Haytham's needs were few. According to another story told by al-Bayhaqi, the Amir-ul-Umara of Syria offered Ibn al-Haytham a large sum of money and an annual salary to work as a scholar in his court. Ibn al-Haytham agreed to perform the service, but not at the price the Syrian leader offered. "All that I need is my daily food, a servant, and a maid to look after me," Ibn al-Haytham said. "If I amass more than the barest minimum that I need, I shall turn into your slave, and, if I spend what I save, I shall be held liable for wasting your wealth."

When not teaching or copying manuscripts, Ibn al-Haytham pursued his own studies. He was finally able to write the long-deferred follow-up to his commentary on _Almagest_. In this new book, _Maqala fi al-Shukuk 'ala Batlamyus_ or _Doubts Concerning Ptolemy_, Ibn al-Haytham uses his understanding of light and vision to discuss not only _Almagest_ but also Ptolemy's _Optics_. He points out a contradiction between the explanations in Ptolemy's two books about how the atmosphere refracts the light of stars. He also criticizes Ptolemy's discussions of optical illusions, convex mirrors, and refraction.

According to three lists of Ibn al-Haytham's books that Ibn Abi Usaybi'ah included with his biography, the Iraqi scholar may have written as many as 182 treatises after his release from captivity in 1021. List I, which Usaybi'ah said he copied from a version in Ibn al-Haytham's own handwriting, covers a period up to February 10, 1027. This list contains a total of sixty-nine works—twenty-five on mathematics and forty-four on philosophy and physics. List I has no beginning date, so some of the works on it may have been written before Ibn al-Haytham was imprisoned. Others were probably written after his release.

List II, which Usaybi'ah said was also in Ibn al-Haytham's own handwriting, covers the period between February 11, 1027 to July 25, 1028. During these eighteen months Ibn al-Haytham composed another twenty-one works, including additional treatises on philosophy and physics as well as works devoted to theology, medicine, optics, and astronomy. Usaybi'ah's third list contains ninety-two works—two more than Lists I and II combined. These works cover a range of topics including optics, mathematics, astronomy, music, poetry, logic, and ethics. List III is important because it is the only list of the three that contains *The Book of Optics*. There is some controversy among historians over whether List III covers only the time between 1028 (the end of List II) and 1038 (the end of Ibn al-Haytham's life), or rather is a catalogue of a number of Ibn al-Haytham's works from throughout his career.

In addition to *The Book of Optics*, Usaybi'ah's List III contains twelve more works on light and vision. In one of these, *Discourse on Light*, the Iraqi scholar summarizes the sections of *The Book of Optics* devoted to light. Referring to *The Book of Optics* by name, Ibn al-Haytham recounts the experiments with "dark chambers" that show light radiates from all points of a luminous body and travels in straight lines through the air until it reaches a facing surface. In *Treatise on the Form of the Eclipse*, Ibn al-Haytham uses the camera obscura to observe "the form of the sun's [or moon's] light." In doing so, he offers a correct explanation of how light traveling through an aperture becomes focused on an opaque body, such as a screen or a wall.

Ibn al-Haytham's interest in refraction led him to discuss how light behaves in the atmosphere in *Treatise on the Rainbow and the Halo*. He also explored the behavior of light in astronomical works such as *Treatise on the Appearance of Stars*, *Treatise on the Lights of the Stars*, *Treatise on What Appears of the Differences in the Heights of the Stars*, and *Treatise on the Light of the Moon*. His fascination with reflection led him to write several more treatises on curved surfaces, including *Treatise on the Burning Sphere, Treatise on Spherical Burning Mirrors*, and *Treatise on Parabolic Burning Mirrors*.

Ibn al-Haytham also wrote several works about astronomy. One of these, *On the Configuration of the World*, is his most ambitious and famous book, next to *The Book of Optics*. In *On the Configuration of the World*, Ibn al-Haytham shows his lifelong commitment to "concepts whose matter are sensible things." He begins by stating that earlier astronomers such as Ptolemy had carefully recorded "the circumstances of the heavenly bodies, their relative ordering, their distances from each other, the magnitude of their bodies, their various positions, the kinds of their motions and the varieties of their shapes."

Although these records and calculations were used to predict the positions of celestial bodies with utmost precision, they did not explain what the celestial bodies actually were or how they moved through the heavens. Instead, they were "based upon the motions of imaginary points on the circumferences of intellected circles." Ptolemy had proposed what is known as an epicyclical system, wherein the planets follow a small orbit called an epicycle that in turn orbits a larger sphere called a deferent. Always the skeptic, Ibn al-Haytham was not satisfied with an abstract, imaginary picture of the universe. The planets and stars are real things, he argued, and any theory of their movement must take this into account.

Ptolemy's failure to provide a practical, sensible theory

of the movement of celestial bodies had troubled Ibn al-Haytham for some time. In *Doubts Concerning Ptolemy,* Ibn al-Haytham raised the issue with Ptolemy:

> The diameter of the epicyclic orb is an imaginary line. An imaginary line does not of its own move with a sensible motion which produces something which exists in the world. Similarly, the plane of an epicyclic orb is an imaginary plane, and an imaginary plane does not move with a sensible motion.

Ptolemy placed the earth at the center of his universe with the planets and stars orbiting around it. This artistic rendition comes from Andreas Cellarius's 1660 Harmonia Macrocosmica. (National Library of Australia)

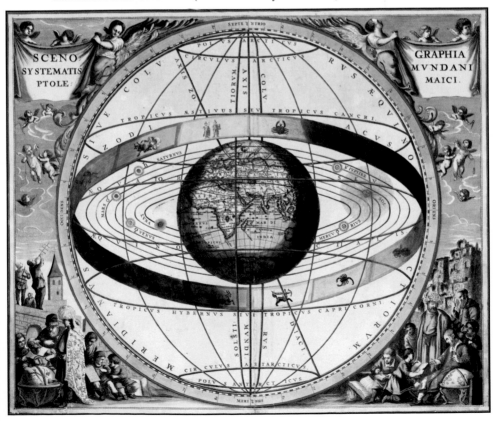

What was needed, Ibn al-Haytham believed, was an explanation of how real, physical bodies move through the sky in a way that conformed to Ptolemy's observations and mathematical calculations. Earlier astronomers had suggested that the heavenly bodies were affixed "to the surfaces of solid spheres," Ibn al-Haytham noted, but these scholars did not explain "the manner by means of which those motions may possibly be consummated." The Iraqi scholar set about the task of explaining "each of the motions which he [Ptolemy] mentioned in such a manner that that motion may appear to be the result of a spherical body that is moving with a simple, continuous, and unceasing motion."

For Ibn al-Haytham, it was vital that the spheres move in a simple, consistent manner. Anything more complicated would violate the laws of nature, as well as human logic. For example, to explain his observations of Mercury and Venus, Ptolemy had suggested that the two planets oscillated, or moved back-and-forth. This explanation, Ibn al-Haytham wrote, violated common sense as well as Ptolemy's earlier statements about the motion of heavenly bodies:

> This is utter nonsense and contradicts his previous doctrine that the heavenly motions are equal, continuous, and unceasing. For it is impossible that anything but a body move with this motion, for only existing [real] bodies can have sensible motions.

Ibn al-Haytham's goal was to describe a system in which all of the heavenly bodies move without "any hindrance, repelling or impediment. Rather their motions, including their combinations, are unceasing and continuous." He pictured a set of spheres, called orbs, nested within each other. "The shape of the world in its entirety is the shape of a sphere," Ibn al-Haytham wrote. "The part surrounding the world and moving around the center is called in its entirety an orb," he continued. "This orb is divided into many parts. It is, however, primarily divided into nine parts, which are contiguous spherical bodies, one of them surrounding the one adjacent to it, the concave surface of the surrounding [orb] touching the convex surface of the one surrounded by it. The center of all these spheres is the center of the world."

Hartmann Schedel's 1493 illustration from his Liber chronicarum *added to al-Haytham's astronomical model, but several core components are the same. For instance, Schedel places the earth at the center with the moon, Mercury, Venus, the sun, Mars, Jupiter, and Saturn contained by the surrounding orbs.* (Huntington Library, San Marino, California)

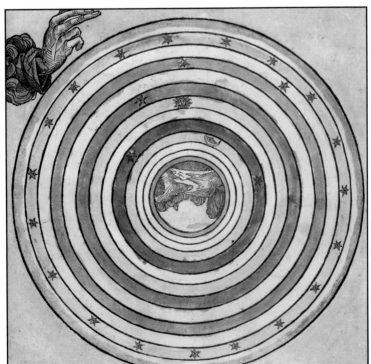

Each orb, he wrote, contains a heavenly body. The nearest orb contained the moon. Moving out from the moon were orbs containing Mercury, Venus, the sun, Mars, Jupiter, Saturn, and, finally, the stars. Beyond the orb containing the stars is "the surrounding greatest orb which sets in motion all these orbs." He then described the motions of all of the orbs in precise geometric terms.

Despite the elegance of his system, Ibn al-Haytham was mostly wrong. The earth does resemble a sphere and the moon does orbit around it; however, the sun, planets, and stars do not revolve around the earth. Rather, the earth and the other planets revolve around the sun, and the sun revolves around the center of the Milky Way galaxy. Nor are the heavenly bodies attached to physical spheres; the paths they travel across the sky are shaped by the invisible force of gravity.

Despite these errors, *On the Configuration of the World* set a new standard for astronomy. No longer would it be acceptable for astronomers to describe the movements of the heavenly bodies with imaginary points and circles. Serious astronomers would have to provide a model of the universe that conformed to astronomical observations and was consistent with the workings of nature. Although Ibn al-Haytham's system proved to be flawed, his insistence that observational data be linked to a realistic planetary scheme anticipated the accomplishments of later astronomers like Nicolaus Copernicus, Galileo Galilei, and Johannes Kepler.

The title of one of Ibn al Haytham's later treatises

offers a tantalizing clue about the last years of his life. The work is called *A Reply by [Ibn al-Haytham] to a Geometrical Question Which He Was Asked at Baghdad in the Months of the Year A.H. 418* [1027–1028 A.D.]. Appearing on Usaybi'ah's List II, this title indicates that Ibn al-Haytham was in Baghdad six years after the death of Caliph al-Hakim. This may not have been the first time Ibn al-Haytham had returned to his home country. A work that appears on Usaybi'ah's List I, *Replies to Seven Mathematical Questions Addressed to Me in Baghdad*, suggests that Ibn al-Haytham had visited the capital of Iraq before 1027 as well, although possibly while he was still living in Basra.

According to Ibn al-Qifti, Ibn al-Haytham spent the last twenty years of his life in Cairo and died there in 1041. Most historians accept this version of the Iraqi scholar's death and claim that his visits to Baghdad were brief. It would not have been unusual for a renowned scholar like Ibn al-Haytham to travel to different cities to meet with other scholars or participate in *munazarah*. On the other hand, Baghdad and Cairo are about nine hundred miles apart. It seems odd that Ibn al-Haytham would have made the 1,800-mile journey from Cairo to Baghdad and back, not just once, but twice, around the age of sixty. His documented presence in Baghdad raises the possibility that the Iraqi scholar may have left Egypt for good, either after being released from captivity in Cairo or, as 'Ali ibn Zayd al-Bayhaqi wrote, immediately after his disastrous meeting with Caliph al-Hakim.

Another clue that Ibn al-Haytham may have lived out his old age in Iraq comes from the oldest surviving manuscript of _The Book of Optics_. The copyist of that manuscript was Ahmad ibn Muhammad ibn Ja'far al-'Askari, the man who claimed in the inscription that he was Ibn al-Haytham's son-in-law. Al-'Askari also says that he completed his copy of the manuscript in Basra. If Ibn al-Haytham died in Cairo, one has to wonder how al-'Askari, living 970 miles away, knew of the existence of the manuscript. Even if he did know about it, it seems highly unlikely that he would have spent several months traveling to Cairo and back to retrieve his father-in-law's book. By all accounts, Ibn al-Haytham was not a wealthy man. Al-'Askari and his wife could not have expected to have earned very much money for such a journey.

The date of al-'Askari's inscription also suggests that Ibn al-Haytham may not have died in Cairo. Al-'Askari says he copied _The Book of Optics_ in 1082, forty-one years after Ibn al-Haytham died. If al-'Askari's wife, Ibn al-Haytham's daughter, was born before the Iraqi scholar left for Egypt around 1010, then she would have been well into her seventies when the copy was made. In all likelihood, al-'Askari was older than his wife. It is doubtful that al-'Askari would have lived to be that old, let alone to have undertaken the task of copying his late father-in-law's enormous manuscript at such an advanced age.

Based on al-'Askari's inscriptions and on Ibn al-Haytham's documented presence in Iraq after 1021, it is possible that Ibn al-Haytham returned to Basra after his

THE KAABA AND THE QIBLA

The Kaaba is the holiest site in Islam. According to the Qur'an, the original Kaaba was built by the ancient patriarch Ibrahim and his son Ismail as a place of prayer, although many dispute this. The building has been leveled and rebuilt several times. It is located inside the Masjid al-Haram mosque in Mecca, in present-day Saudi Arabia. Built of granite and roughly cube-shaped (the word *Kaaba*, in Arabic, is derivative of the word "cube"), the Kaaba is traditionally covered with a gold-embroidered sheet of black silk called the *kiswah*, which is replaced annually. Surrounding the Kaaba for several miles in all directions is a restricted area known as the *harem*, covering most of Mecca, wherein non-Muslims are forbidden. The Kaaba forms an important part of the *hajj*, or pilgrimage to Mecca, that all solvent, able-bodied Muslims are obliged to make at least once in the course of their lifetimes. One ritual of the *hajj* is the *tawaf*, where believers circumambulate the Kaaba seven times in a counterclockwise direction.

Muslims also pray, or *salat*, five times a day in the direction of the Kaaba. This direction—from any given location on the planet toward the Kaaba—is known as the *Qibla*. In Ibn al-Haytham's day, Muslims determined the *Qibla* using a medieval navigational tool called an astrolabe. The Persian philosopher and mathematician (and contemporary of Ibn al-Haytham) Abu Rayhan Biruni used lines of longitude to devise a way to determine the *Qibla* mathematically. These calculations were likely used to devise *Qibla* maps later on. There is still some controversy among Muslims as to the correct way to determine the *Qibla*. Because of the curvature of the Earth, a direct, straight path between the Kaaba and a given location is most often not the shortest path along the Earth's surface. Some Muslims pray in the direction of a "great circle" route (the shortest path) while others pray along a "rhumb line" (the direct path).

trip to Egypt. If he did so at age forty-six, immediately after his meeting with Caliph al-Hakim, or even at fifty-six, after being released from captivity, he certainly would have been young enough to father al-'Askari's wife. If he was not married before he left for Egypt, he may have married for the first time when he returned. Since Muslim men were allowed to have up to four wives, Ibn al-Haytham could also have taken a second wife or married more than one woman when he returned to Iraq. If Ibn al-Haytham's daughter was born after he returned to Basra, she would have been between the ages of forty and sixty when her husband copied _The Book of Optics_—a much more reasonable scenario.

Whether Ibn al-Haytham spent his last years unmarried in Cairo, the scholarly hermit of legend, or married with a daughter and son-in-law in Basra, his life came to an end around 1040. According to al-Bayhaqi, the elderly Ibn al-Haytham developed a persistent case of diarrhea. Despite intense pain, the Iraqi scholar clung to life for seven long days. Finally, feeling his life ebbing away, the man who began his career by studying religion turned towards the Kaaba, the holy shrine in Mecca that Muslims face when they pray, and recited a verse from the Qur'an: "Verily my return is to Thee; I rely upon Thee and turn unto Thee." With these words, the greatest scientist of the Middle Ages left the world he had worked so hard to understand and to explain to others. Ibn al-Haytham's life was over, but the revolution he founded had scarcely begun.

SEVEN

"The Physicist"

Just as many of the key facts of Ibn al-Haytham's life remain shrouded in mystery, so too do many of the events that occurred after his death. For example, *The Book of Optics* was translated into Latin in the late twelfth or early thirteen century, but the identity of the translator is unknown. Also, according to Ibn Abi Usaybi'ah, Ibn al-Haytham wrote at least 182 books and treatises. In his autobiography, Ibn al-Haytham wrote that several more of his works had "fallen into the hands of certain people in Basra and Ahwaz, the prototypes of which have been lost." Of the approximately two hundred works that Ibn al-Haytham composed in his lifetime, only about a third—sixty-two works—are known to have survived to the present day. The fate of the other two-thirds of Ibn al-Haytham's output remains a mystery.

Many of Ibn-al Haytham's missing works may have been deliberately destroyed. Even within Ibn al-Haytham's lifetime, religious leaders looked upon some fields of learning with suspicion. These leaders were guided in their thinking by the Prophet Muhammad's saying, "May God protect us from useless knowledge." Only knowledge that led Muslims toward God was valid. All other knowledge was excessive and potentially dangerous.

In this spirit, higher mathematics and the natural sciences were not taught within mosques when Ibn al-Haytham was himself a student. After Ibn al-Haytham's death, traditionalists began to express even greater hostility toward the subjects the Iraqi scholar had spent a lifetime exploring. "The problems of physics are of no importance for us in our religious affairs and our livelihoods," wrote the fourteenth-century historian Ibn Khaldun. "Therefore we must leave them alone." Another prominent religious leader, Ibn al-Salah Al-Shahrazuri, was even more peremptory. Two hundred years after Ibn al-Haytham's death, Ibn al-Salah issued a *fatwa*, or legal opinion on Islamic law, condemning the study of philosophical sciences. "Philosophy was the foundation of foolishness," al-Salah declared. "Logic is the introduction to philosophy, and the introduction to evil is evil."

The process that led to the condemnation and censorship of Ibn al-Haytham's works did not occur everywhere at the same time. His works circulated throughout the Arabic-speaking world, into areas controlled by many different sects. Attitudes toward philosophy and science varied from

Moses Maimonides, who was 13 years old when Córdoba fell under the control of Islamic extremists, escaped to Egypt with his family after refusing to become a Muslim. He quickly gained a reputation as a gifted physician. Maimonides served as personal physician to Saladin's vizier and refused a similar position with England's Richard I. In his lifetime he produced many important works on medicine, philosophy, and astronomy. (Jewish Encyclopedia)

city to city. According to the writings of a student of Moses Maimonides, an important Jewish philosopher who died in Egypt in 1204, the suppression of philosophical works was well underway in Baghdad by the beginning of the thirteenth century. The student wrote that he saw Baghdad officials burn the library of a philosopher who had died in 1214. It is not known if any of Ibn al-Haytham's books or treatises were part of that philosopher's collection, but eventually some of Ibn al-Haytham's works met the same fate.

Critics of "useless knowledge" did not drive science out of Muslim society altogether. Science that was useful to attaining spiritual ends continued to have a place. In the thirteenth century, for example, religious leaders began to employ a person to calculate the times of the five daily prayers each day. The person who performed these calculations was known as the *muwaqqit*, from the Arabic word *waqt*, which means "definite time." The times of the daily prayers were traditionally linked to the movements of the sun, such as sunrise and sunset, so the *muwaqqit*

THE JEWISH DIASPORA

Long before the early Christians left Judea, many Jews were already living outside its border. Thousands of Jews were taken to Babylonia, in what is now Iraq, to serve as slaves in 586 B.C. The Jews were allowed to return to their native land in 538 B.C., but many decided to stay behind in what became known as the first Jewish Diaspora. Over the next few centuries, trade, scholarship, and other activities drew more Jews away from their homeland. Many others were sold into slavery. In the first century B.C., Jews made up forty percent of the population of the Egyptian city of Alexandria. After Romans sacked Jerusalem in 70 A.D., many more Jews left Judea. By the end of the first century, five million Jews lived outside their homeland, outnumbering those who lived in it.

The Romans permitted the Jews a certain amount freedom to practice their religion, but these freedoms slowly eroded under Christian rulers before and after the fall of the Roman Empire. By the Middle Ages, Christians in some parts of Europe denied Jews citizenship and barred them from professional associations known as guilds. By the twelfth century, Jews in some parts of Europe were forced to live in specific sections of cities and towns, which became known as ghettos. Despite the oppression, Jews preserved their culture and religion and many excelled as scholars, philosophers, and writers.

had to be both an astronomer and a mathematician. Some *muwaqqits*, such as the medieval astronomer Ibn al-Shatir, went beyond their normal duties to make new discoveries. Most, however, did not.

As interest in pure science waned in the Muslim world, the opposite was happening in Europe. For centuries, scholars in Europe had studied only those subjects that pertained to their own religion, Christianity. Founded by Jesus of Nazareth, Christianity spread from its birthplace in Judea, a province of the Roman Empire, throughout the areas bordering the Mediterranean Sea. Suppressed for hundreds of years by leaders of the Roman Empire, Christianity became the official religion of Rome in the fourth century. With the support of the Roman Empire, Christianity spread north through Europe and east through Asia Minor.

Like the Muslims, the Christians believed that the purpose of earthly life was to live according to God's revealed laws and teachings. As in the Muslim world, most education in Christendom took place in the churches and centered on religious thought. Christianity's greatest thinkers were theologians and philosophers. By the twelfth century, however, Christian scholars were beginning to broaden their interests to other areas, including the realm of science.

The only area of medieval Europe that had eluded the grasp of Christendom was Spain, which remained under Muslim rule. Like Muslims throughout the world, the rulers of Spain believed that Jews and Christians were both *Ahl al-Kitab*, or "People of the Book." According to Muslim theology, non-Muslims who revered sacred books, such as the Jewish Torah and the Christian Bible, were different from other non-Muslims, who were considered to be nonbelievers or heathens.

The Muslims believed that the ancient Jewish prophets were divinely inspired and that the books that told of their revelations were holy. "We believe in Allah and that which is revealed to us and that which was revealed unto Abraham and Ishmael and Isaac and Jacob and the tribes, and that which was vouchsafed unto Moses and Jesus and the prophets from their Lord. We make no distinction between any of them, and to Him we have surrendered," reads a verse of the Qur'an. Because of their closeness to God, People of the Book were not required to convert to Islam, and Muslim leaders were bound by faith not to interfere with their worship. "He who wrongs a Jew or a Christian will have myself as his indicter on the day of judgment," Muhammad declared.

Although relations between Spanish Muslims, Christians, and Jews were by no means always peaceful, a general atmosphere of tolerance prevailed, making Spain a vibrant center of learning. In Toledo, Córdoba, and other Spanish cities, Muslim, Jewish, and Christian scholars exchanged views and shared information. Through the Muslims, Jewish and Christian scholars came into contact with the works of the ancient Greeks, which had been preserved in Arabic translations. They also discovered the works of Muslim scholars such as al-Khwarizmi, Ibn al-Kindi, and Ibn al-Haytham.

Construction on the great mosque of Córdoba, Spain, began in 784 and ended in 987. At that time, it stood as the second-largest mosque in the world. It remains one of the most impressive examples of Islamic architecture in Spain, despite its reconsecration as a Christian church in 1236. (Courtesy of North Wind Pictures.)

Word of the Muslim libraries gradually spread beyond the borders of Spain. In the twelfth century, for example, an Italian named Gerard of Cremona wanted to read Ptolemy's *Almagest*, an oft-praised but little-read book that had not been available in a Latin translation for centuries. Gerard heard, however, that an Arabic translation of the Greek astronomer's book was available in the Spanish city of Toledo. Gerard traveled to Toledo, learned Arabic, and read the book.

Once in Toledo, Gerard discovered works by other Greeks that also had been translated into Arabic. Rather than returning to Italy, Gerard stayed in Spain and began translating Arabic books into Latin. In addition to

Almagest, Gerard translated books by Aristotle, Euclid, and Galen. Gerard soon found that Muslim scholars had not only preserved the works of the ancient Greeks, but had also commented on them, expanded on them, and even surpassed them with their discoveries. He began to translate books by Muslim scholars such as the Iranian physician Abu 'Ali al-Husayn ibn 'Abd Allah ibn Sina, known in Latin as Avicenna.

As Gerard of Cremona began to grasp the extent of Muslim knowledge, he realized that he could not translate all of the important Arabic books by himself. He began to recruit other scholars to help translate the treasures of Muslim learning. Just as Caliph al-Ma'mun had founded the House of Wisdom in Baghdad four hundred years earlier to translate the works of the Greeks, Gerard of Cremona founded a center in Toledo to translate the works of Muslim scholars. In all, Gerard and his followers translated more than eighty Arabic works into Latin. One of those works was *On Parabolic Burning Mirrors* by Ibn al-Haytham.

Many of the twelfth- and thirteenth-century European translators working at Gerard's center did not sign their manuscripts. Such was the case of the translator who came across a massive Arabic text entitled *Kitab al-Manazir*. The anonymous scholar translated the title of this work as *De aspectibus*, or *The Optics*. He called the author Alhacen, a Latinized form of al-Hasan. *De aspectibus* fascinated medieval European scholars. They were impressed with its novel ideas about vision, its detailed account of the anatomy of the eye, and its description of experiments that any person could duplicate. It became one of the most copied works of medieval Muslim science.

The Latin translation of *Kitab al-Manazir* is far from perfect. Rather than quoting Ibn al-Haytham, the translator often paraphrases him. Because of the translator's lack of knowledge about optics, the paraphrased sections can be misleading. The translator also condensed the book by leaving out whole passages. For example, the translator includes the camera obscura experiment in Book I that involves a screen, but he leaves out the following experiment with the two-panel door. Perhaps most grievously, he also omits the entire first three chapters of Book I.

Whether the Latin translator skipped the first three chapters, or the Arabic manuscript he used did not contain them in the first place, the readers of *De aspectibus* missed out on vital information. The Iraqi scholar's description of the two earlier theories of vision; his initial observations and conclusions about the nature and properties of light; his elegant thoughts on the difficulty of achieving certainty in matters of science; his entire method of inquiry—all of these important points were left out.

Because of these omissions, European scholars were not able to fully understand Ibn al-Haytham's theories of light, especially his description of how it radiates from primary and secondary sources. Without this basic information, European scholars often appended their own theories to support those of Ibn al-Haytham. Unfortunately, some scholars used popular ideas about how living creatures multiply to explain the propagation of light. The inclusion of these apocryphal explanations in *De aspectibus* caused confusion for years to come.

Even without the first three chapters, however, many of Ibn al-Haytham's revolutionary ideas came through to European readers. Because he often alludes to earlier portions of his book, some of the observations and conclusions contained in the first three chapters of Book I are mentioned later. Ibn al-Haytham's method, although not explicitly spelled out in the original Latin translation, is evident throughout the book.

One of the first medieval scholars to read and respond to Ibn al-Haytham's masterpiece was a Franciscan monk named Roger Bacon. Born into a prosperous family around 1220 in England, Bacon may well have been schooled in Latin and arithmatic by a local priest. He enrolled in the University of Oxford at the age of thirteen—the common age to start a university education at that time. After receiving a master of arts degree from Oxford and briefly joining the faculty of the university, Bacon moved to Paris in 1241 and remained there for six years, lecturing on Aristotle at the University of Paris. There he met Peter Peregrinus of Maricourt, the author of the earliest known treatise on magnets and magnetism. This meeting appears to have changed not only the course of Bacon's life, but the history of European science as well.

Bacon returned to Oxford and devoted himself to the study of optics, astronomy, mathematics, and alchemy, a chemical science and speculative philosophy that aimed to transform common metals into gold, as well as to

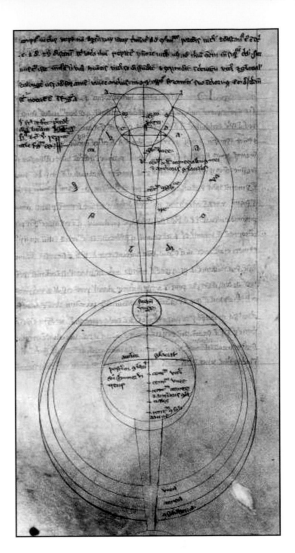

This folio from Bacon's Perspectiva, *published in the late 13th century, uses diagrams to illustrate optical theories that closely mirror al-Haytham's.* (British Library)

discover a universal cure for disease and a way to prolong life indefinitely. One of the books in Bacon's collection appears to have been *De aspectibus*. Bacon wrote a book about optics entitled *Perspectiva* closely based on Ibn al-Haytham's work.

Bacon accepted Ibn al-Haytham's theories about light and repeated some of his experiments, including the one with a camera obscura. Most importantly, Bacon endorsed the Iraqi scholar's method of inquiry. Throughout his writings,

Bacon stressed the importance of experimentation in the discovery of scientific truth. Throughout Europe during Bacon's time, a movement called Scholasticism was gaining strength that aimed to reconcile classical knowledge with Christian theology. Scholasticism based its teachings largely on consultation with authorities like Aristotle and the Church. Although he admired Aristotle, Bacon believed that knowledge should be pursued independently, without the influence of previously maintained dogmas. Bacon may have taken his cues from Ibn al-Haytham, who also revered Aristotle but wrote *The Book of Optics* without reference to other thinkers, establishing all of his conclusions on the basis of experimentation, observation, mathematics, and deduction.

Although Bacon acknowledged his debt to Ibn al-Haytham in the field of optics, he did not give the Iraqi scholar credit for having developed the method of inquiry that he so strongly advanced. Instead, Bacon praised Peter Peregrinus as the *dominus experimentorum,* or the master of experiments. "[Peregrinus] gains knowledge of matters of nature, medicine, and alchemy through experiment," Bacon wrote, "and all that is in the heaven and in the earth beneath."

Bacon may have credited Peregrinus over Ibn al-Haytham for pioneering the experimental method because he knew the Frenchman personally and revered his work. He also may have had another motive. Bacon and Peregrinus were devout Christians at a time when Christians and Muslims were fighting for control of Jerusalem and the areas around it in a series of wars known as the Crusades. Bacon was a member of the clergy and Peregrinus had even fought in one of the Crusades himself. Because of these ongoing conflicts, Bacon may have felt that attaching a Muslim scholar's name to the scientific method would slow its acceptance among Christians.

Another Franciscan friar deeply impressed with *De aspectibus* was John Pecham. Ten years younger than Bacon, Pecham was born in Sussex, England, around 1230 and educated at the University of Paris. He was so inspired by *De aspectibus* that he decided to summarize it, much as Ibn al-Haytham had once summarized the works of Ptolemy and Euclid. Pecham patterned his book, *Perspectiva communis*, after *De aspectibus,* and he frequently references Ibn al-Haytham, whom he calls "the Author" or "the Physicist."

While Pecham was condensing Ibn al-Haytham's work, another European scholar was expanding on it. Erazmus Ciolek Witelo, commonly known as just Witelo, was a friar of the Roman Catholic Church who attended college in the Italian city of Padua around 1260. He later traveled to the Italian city of Viterbo where he met William of Moerbeke, a renowned translator of Aristotle. At some point, Witelo came across *De aspectibus*. Like Bacon and Pecham, Witelo was impressd with Ibn al-Haytham's work. He decided to write his own book on optics, which he called *Perspectiva* and dedicated to William of Moerbeke. Although Witelo does not cite Ibn al-Haytham by name, the structure of his *Perspectiva* is identical to the organization of *De aspectibus*. The content is similar as well. Through Bacon,

Pecham, and Witelo, Ibn al-Haytham's ideas and methods spread through Europe.

Scholars continued to read Ibn al-Haytham's work independently of his European commentators, as well. At the beginning of the fourteenth century, _De aspectibus_ was translated from Latin—the language of scholars—into Italian, the common language of the Italian people. This translation made Ibn al-Haytham's discoveries available to people in trades and business. The Italian sculptor Lorenzo Ghiberti reported having read _The Book of Optics_. Ghiberti sculpted a pair of magnificent doors for the baptistery of the Florence Cathedral, earning him great acclaim for his lifelike figures and strong sense of spatial depth.

Ghiberti won the right to install his bronze doors in Florence Cathedral's baptistery in a 1401 contest. This panel shows Adam and Eve in Eden. Ghiberti's doors received their unofficial name, the Gates of Paradise, from Michelangelo who painted the Sistine Chapel. (Battistero di San Giovanni, Florence)

Ghiberti was not the only artist to suddenly figure out how to create the illusion of three-dimensional space on a flat surface. All across Europe, artists began to create realistic perspective in paintings, drawings, and shallow relief sculptures. The people and animals in these works seemed more solid and alive than those in earlier works. Dutch artists—such as Jan Vermeer and Jan van Eyck—also began reproduce elaborate details, such as the lace on clothing and tablecloths, with photographic realism. These advances were doubtlessly attended by a more precise, scientific understanding of vision and light, like that sought by Ibn al-Haytham. But recent scholarship has also suggested that Ibn al-Haytham may have contributed in a more direct way, through his most famous invention: the camera obscura. Many scholars have suggested that the Dutch Masters used cameras obscura to project three-dimensional scenes onto flat surfaces and then traced the images.

Whether or not *The Book of Optics* played a role in revolutionizing European art, the fame of its author continued to grow. In 1572 a Swiss publisher named Frederick Risner published *De aspectibus* and Witelo's *Perspectiva* together in one book called *Opticae thesaurus*. The two earlier books were so similar that Risner used several of the same illustrations for both texts and included many cross-references between them. Through Risner, thousands of scholars and students across Europe became familiar with Ibn al-Haytham's methods and ideas.

By the time Risner published the *Opticae thesaurus,* Europe was in the middle of a period of discovery and

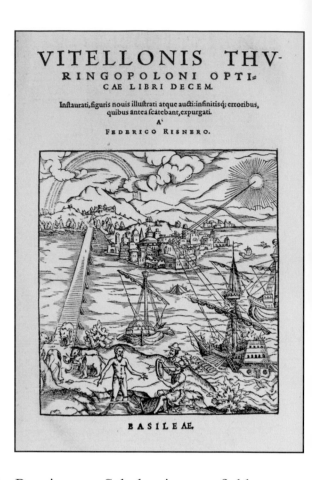

Risner's 1572 Opticae thesaurus _included a Latin translation of al-Haytham's_ The Book of Optics. _Risner's frontispiece uses a rainbow, a bridge vanishing into the distance, a man whose legs appear bent in water, and Archimedes's trick of using mirrors to burn enemy ships to illustrate properties of light and vision._ (University of Oklahoma)

learning known as the Renaissance. Scholars in many fields made tremendous advances. For example, in 1543 the Polish astronomer Nicolaus Copernicus proposed the theory that the earth rotated on its own axis every twenty-four hours and that it and the other planets revolved around the sun. In 1572, the same year Risner published Ibn al-Haytham's work, the Danish astronomer Tycho Brahe observed the birth of a new star in the constellation Cassiopeia, a finding that challenged the widespread belief that the stars were permanently fixed in the sky. In 1610 the Italian mathematician and astronomer Galileo Galilei used the newly invented telescope to discover four moons revolving around Jupiter—a discovery that helped to confirm the Copernican model of orbiting planets and moons. Galileo also used mathematics and experimentation to prove wrong many of Aristotle's theories about motion. He was another prominent advocate of experimental science.

As scientific learning in Europe increased, so did appreciation and recognition of Ibn al-Haytham. For the first time, Europeans had the skills to fully appreciate the higher mathematics contained in *The Book of Optics*. Seventeenth-century mathematicians such as Pierre de Fermat of France, Thomas Harriot of England, Isaac Beeckman and Willebrord van Roijen Snell of the Netherlands, and Johannes Kepler of Germany all referred to Alhazen by name in their works.

Kepler used Ibn al-Haytham's own methods to disprove one of the Iraqi scholar's theories about vision. Kepler filled a glass sphere with water to represent an eye filled with fluids. He then placed the glass sphere near the aperture of a camera obscura and observed the result. He found that the rays entering through the aperture were bent by the glass and the fluid in a way that created a "*pictura*," or image—upside down and backwards—on the back of the sphere. This experiment led Kepler to propose that the eye works like a camera obscura, with the pupil serving as an aperture and the retina as the receiving screen. The optic nerve carries the image from the retina to the brain, which inverts the image so that it perceives objects right side up.

JOHANNES KEPLER

The German mathematician and scientist Johannes Kepler, who was responsible for correcting many of Ibn al-Haytham's mistakes about optics, also made important contributions to astronomy. Kepler was born in 1571 in the central German city of Weil der Stadt. He was a precocious youth who showed a strong interest in astronomy and astrology, but a childhood bout of smallpox left his vision weak and unsuited for accurately viewing the heavens. He committed himself to the theoretical and mathematical aspects of astronomy rather than observation.

While studying astronomy and mathematics at the University of Tübingen, Kepler became convinced that the sun-centered, or heliocentric, model of the universe proposed by the Polish astronomer Nicolaus Copernicus was correct. After graduating from Tübingen and briefly teaching mathematics and astronomy at a Protestant school in Graz, Austria, Kepler was invited to join the Danish astronomer Tycho Brahe at his observatory outside of Prague. Tycho was the imperial astronomer of the Holy Roman Empire, and was compiling the most accurate and extensive stellar observations ever made.

Kepler spent only a year with Tycho, but upon Tycho's death in 1601, he succeeded the Dane as imperial astronomer and set to work trying to produce a planetary scheme that would explain the wealth of raw data he inherited from Tycho. After working with circular orbits for years, Kepler stumbled upon the idea that the planets travel in elliptical orbits. Known as Kepler's first law of planetary motion, this was a revolutionary idea in the history of astronomy. Ever since the time of Aristotle, circular motion had been the sacrosanct rule of planetary motion. Ibn al-Haytham had endorsed the idea of circular orbits himself in his astronomical treatises _Doubts Concerning Ptolemy_ and _On the Configuration_ *of the World*. Kepler's other two laws of planetary motion, which explained the speed of the planets on their orbits, helped lead Isaac Newton to discover the universal law of gravitation.

In addition to his scientific interests, Kepler was also a deeply religious and mystical man. He made horoscopes for his patron, Holy Roman Emperor Rudolph II, and believed that the movements of planets operated on the same principles that governed musical harmony and mathematics. Many of his arguments were theological rather than scientific. After Rudolph II's death in 1612, Kepler left Prague and took a post as a provincial mathematician in Linz, Austria. He died in 1630.

For more than six hundred years—two hundred years longer than the period from Galileo's death to today—Ibn al-Haytham had reigned as the world's leading authority in several fields. By the middle of the seventeenth century, however, European scientists had refined, expanded on, and surpassed most of his discoveries. In 1637, for example, the French scientist and mathematician René Descartes, who had read *The Book of Optics*, published three essays— *Dioptrics*, *Meteorology*, and *Geometry*—that expanded on Ibn al-Haytham's discoveries regarding refraction, the rainbow, and analytic geometry. The Dutch physicist Christian Huygens also read Ibn al-Haytham's masterpiece and answered many of its unsolved questions.

Although no longer hailed as "the Physicist," Ibn al-Haytham was still revered as one of the founders of modern science. When the Polish astronomer Johannes Hevelius published a detailed description of the moon's surface in 1647, the publisher hired an artist to design an illustration

In the frontispiece to Hevelius's Selenographia, *Ibn al-Haytham represents Ratione (the use of reason) with his geometrical proof and Galileo represents Sensu (the use of the senses) with his telescope. The two scientists hold the book's title page between them, suggesting a harmony between the methods.* (University of Oklahoma)

for the frontispiece of the book. The engraving shows two standing figures holding a large scroll bearing the title of the book, *Selenographia*. One of the figures is Galileo; the other is Ibn al-Haytham. Galileo holds a telescope, a symbol of observation. Ibn al-Haytham holds a geometrical drawing, a symbol of mathematical proof. The two men and the objects they hold represent two steps of the scientific method that both men pioneered.

Four years after Hevelius honored Ibn al-Haytham on the frontispiece of his lunar atlas, another scientist went a step further: he put the Iraqi scholar's name a map of the moon. In 1651 a Jesuit priest named Gianbattista Riccioli published a book entitled *Almagestum Novum* that included new maps of the lunar surface. Riccioli began the tradition of naming craters after scientists and other scholars. He named one of most prominent craters for Copernicus, and two others for Galileo and Kepler. He reserved some sections of his map for ancient Greeks, some for ancient Romans, some for his contemporaries, and some for medieval and Arabic scholars. About fifteen degrees north of the Moon's equator, just to the east of Mare Crisium, stands a circular impact crater about thirty kilometers wide. Riccioli named this crater Alhazen. In 1935 the International Astronomical Union (IAU), the internationally recognized authority for naming celestial bodies and their surface features, standardized the names of six hundred lunar features, including the crater Riccioli had named for Ibn al-Haytham.

With the passage of time, Ibn al-Haytham's name and achievements faded into history, but around the beginning of the twentieth century things began to change. Scholars such as Carl Brockelmann, Heinrich Suter, and Eilhard Wiedemann—all from Germany—traveled to Istanbul and other centers of Muslim learning and unearthed long-forgotten works by the Iraqi scholar. In 1936 Max Krause, another German scholar, published a list of manuscript copies of *Kitab al-Manazir* that included a reference to the manuscript that had been copied by Ibn al-Haytham's son-in-law, ibn Ja'far al-'Askari. Since then, scholars have translated the complete *Kitab al-Manazir*—including the three chapters missing from the Latin translation—into the major European languages. Many of his other works, including *On the Configuration of the World* and *Completion of the Conics of Apollonius* also have been translated into Western languages. For the first time in centuries, scholars began to appreciate the breadth of Ibn al-Haytham's knowledge.

Ibn al-Haytham's reputation rose in the Arab world as well. When French troops under the leadership of Napoleon Bonaparte occupied Egypt in 1798, Muslim scholars began to fully appreciate how far behind the Europeans they had fallen. "Our country must change its ways, and new sciences must be introduced," declared Sheik Hassan al-'Attar, after examining the technology the French brought to Cairo. When the Ottoman leader Muhammad 'Ali became the viceroy of Egypt in 1805, he began to modernize Egyptian education. In 1836 'Ali proposed an educational mission to France to gather information about modern military technology, engineering, medicine, physical science, and mathematics. Sheik 'Attar, then rector of the Azhar Mosque, recommended his former pupil, Rifa 'a Rafi al-Tahtawi, lead the mission. Upon his return from Europe, al-Tahtawi became the director of the School of Languages, an institution devoted the translation and study of scientific works. As Muslim students and teachers absorbed the lessons of European science, they came to appreciate the role Muslim scholars such as Ibn al-Haytham had played in the scientific revolution of the Renaissance.

Napoleon Bonaparte in Cairo. (Courtesy of North Wind Pictures.)

As the millennial anniversary of Ibn al-Haytham's birth approached, scholars around the world prepared to honor one of the foremost founders of modern science. The nation of Pakistan issued a special stamp commemorating Ibn al-Haytham as the "Father of Optics." In 1969 the Hamdard

National Foundation, a charitable organization founded with proceeds from the Hamdard medical laboratories, sponsored a celebration of the one-thousandth anniversary of Ibn al-Haytham's birth. Scientists and historians traveled to the University of Karachi, in Karachi, Pakistan, to deliver papers and discuss the Iraqi scholar's legacy.

Their scientific heritage reclaimed and renewed, Muslims around the world celebrated the memory of Ibn al-Haytham in public life. In 1971 the nation of Qatar issued a postage stamp honoring Ibn al-Haytham as part of the "Famous Men of Islam" series. Leaders in the Hashemite Kingdom of Jordan named a hospital in Amman after the Iraqi scholar. Not far from where Ibn al-Haytham took part in _munazarah_ stands the Ibn al-Haytham College of Education, part of the University of Baghdad. Children in central Baghdad attend Ibn al-Haytham Elementary School, while boys in the Palestinian city of Nablus attend the Ibn al-Haytham Elementary School for Boys. On April 4, 1992, Saddam Hussein, the former leader of Iraq, established the Ibn Al Haytham Missile Research and Design Center, dedicated to the development of ballistic missiles.

Ibn al-Haytham has been featured on Iraqi currency at various times in history. In 1931 the government of Iraq began issuing a new banknote, the dinar, to replace the Indian rupee as the official currency of Iraq. The new banknotes featured images of Iraqi landmarks and historical figures, including Ibn al-Haytham. After the first Persian Gulf War in 1991, the government of Iraq issued new currency. A portrait of Saddam Hussein replaced the image of

Ibn al-Haytham and one of his geometrical proofs on the Iraqi 10,000-dinar bank note.

Ibn al-Haytham on the 10-dinar note. After a coalition of forces led by the United States deposed Saddam Hussein in 2003, the Iraqis formed a new government. On October 15, 2003, the Central Bank of Iraq issued new currency based on the old banknote designs. The Central Bank decided to decorate the face of the new 10,000-dinar note—the second-largest denomination in the new currency—with a portrait of Ibn al-Haytham, Iraq's greatest scientist, as a symbol of progress and achievement for the new nation.

Were he alive today, Ibn al-Haytham no doubt would applaud the goals and aspirations of modern science, but he would have cautioned students and scholars every-where to regard all sources of information, including his own works, with a healthy skepticism. "Truth is sought for itself, but the truths are immersed in uncertainties, and scientific authorities are not immune from error, nor is human nature itself," he wrote in *Doubts Concerning Ptolemy*. He continued:

> The seeker after truth is not one who studies the writings of the ancients and, following his natural disposition, puts his trust in them, but rather the one who suspects his faith in them and questions what he gathers from them, the one who submits to argument and demonstration, and not to the sayings of a human being whose nature is fraught with all kinds of imperfection and deficiency. Thus the job of the man who investigates the writings of scientists, if learning the truth is his goal, is to make himself an enemy of all that he reads, and applying his mind to the core and margins of its content, attack it from every side. He should also suspect himself as he performs his critical examination of it, so that he may avoid falling into either prejudice or leniency.

timeline

965	Abu 'Ali al-Hasan ibn al-Hasan ibn al-Haytham is born in Basra, in what is now Iraq.
circa 975	Attends school in the local mosque.
c. 985	Begins theological studies in earnest.
c. 990	Abandons theology; discovers the works of Aristotle.
c. 995	Studies and begins to write commentaries on the work of Greek mathematicians.
c. 1000	Appointed to a government post in Basra; writes books on practical subjects such as measurement, the construction of water clocks, and astronomy; suggests a plan to dam the Nile.
c.1005	Shows signs of mental illness; relieved from government post.
1010	Receives summons from Fatimid Caliph al-Hakim.
1011	Travels to Egypt and meets Caliph al-Hakim; according to one account, travels to Aswan and assesses the feasibility of building a dam on the Nile; reports his findings to al-Hakim in Cairo; admits failure; is given a government post; shows signs of mental illness; is placed under house arrest.
1011–1021	Living in isolation under house arrest, probably composes some or all of *The Book of Optics*.
1021	Death of Caliph al-Hakim; released from house arrest; begins writing new books and treatises.
1027	Writes a brief autobiography.
c. 1027	Travels to Baghdad and participates in a *munazarah*.
1028–1040	Composes as many as ninety-two new works, including twelve about light and vision.
c. 1040	Dies after a persistent case of diarrhea.

sources

CHAPTER ONE: Boyhood in Basra

p. 11, "When inquiry concerns . . ." Ibn al-Haytham, *The Optics of Ibn al-Haytham*, trans. A. I. Sabra (London: The Warburg Institute, 1989), 3–4.

p. 11, "The premises are . . ." Ibid., 3.

p. 14, "Those who remember . . ." *The Qur'an*, The Family of Imran, verse 191.

p. 14, "Seeking knowledge is . . ." "Ten Misconceptions about Islam," USC-MSA Compendium of Muslim Texts, http://www.usc.edu/dept/MSA/notislam/misconceptions.html (accessed June 20, 2006).

p. 17, "called by the people . . ." *Encyclopaedia Britannica Online*, s.v. "The Thousand and One Nights," http://www.britannica.com/eb/article-9072265 (accessed August 4, 2005).

CHAPTER TWO: Scholar of Basra

p. 27, "I decided to discover . . ." Dr. Naseer Ahmad Nasir, "Ibn al-Haitham and His Philosophy," in *Ibn al-Haitham; Proceedings of the Celebrations of 1000ᵗʰ Anniversary*, edited by Hakim Mohammed Said (Sadar, Pakistan: The Times Press, 1969), 82.

p. 27, "truth is a unitary entity," Ibid.

p. 27, "From my very . . . of its faith," Ibid.

p. 31, "the consolidated majority," *Encyclopaedia Britannica Online*, s.v. "Islam," http://www.britannica.com/eb/article-69166 (accessed August 25, 2005).

p. 31, "Having gained an . . . spell and skepticism," Nasir, "Ibn al-Haitham and His Philosophy," 82.

p. 32, "I have . . . begun . . .," Ibid.

p. 32, "I studied in . . .way to Reality," Ibid.

p. 32, "When I discovered . . ." Ibid.

p. 34, "Aristotle has discussed . . . truth and falsehood," Ibid.

p. 34, "I saw that I . . ." Saleh Beshara Omar, *Ibn al-Hyatham's Optics* (Minneapolis: Bibliotheca Islamica, 1977), 13.

p. 34, "I found such theories . . ." Nasir, "Ibn al-Haitham and his Philosophy," 82.

p. 34, "It became my belief . . ." Ibid.

p. 34, "There are three disciplines . . ." Ibid.

p. 36, "Should God out of . . ." Ibid., 88.

p. 37, "a thesaurus of . . . exponents of algebra," Ibid., 87.

p. 38, "I have not been . . . mathematical disciplines thoroughly," Ibid., 86.

CHAPTER THREE: "Madness"

p. 41, "This work is extremely . . . "Abdul Ghafur Chaudhri, "Ibn al-Haitham: The Educational and Scientific Importance of his Writings" in *Ibn al-Haitham; Proceedings of the Celebrations of 1000th Anniversary*, edited by Hakim Mohammed Said (Sadar, Pakistan: The Times Press, 1969), 116.

p. 43, "a book on civil . . ." Nasir, "Ibn al-Haitham and His Philosophy," 93.

p. 43, "Had I been . . . its ebb and flow," Serajul Haque, PhD, "A Peep into the Life and Works of Ibn al-Haitham" in *Ibn al-Haitham; Proceedings of the Celebrations of 1000th Anniversary*, edited by Hakim Mohammed Said (Sadar, Pakistan: The Times Press, 1969), 171.

p. 44, "I am not aware . . . any of the three," Nasir, "Ibn al-Haitham and His Philosophy," 82.

CHAPTER FOUR: To Egypt

p. 52, "You are wrong . . ." Nasir, "Ibn al-Haitham and His Philosophy," 93.

p. 52, "At this, Abu Ali . . ." Ibid.

p. 54, "out of fear . . ." A. I. Sabra, Introduction to _The Optics of Ibn al-Haytham_, xix.

CHAPTER FIVE: Scholar of Cairo

p. 58, "followed persuasive methods . . . should be discarded," Ibn al-Haytham, _The Optics of Ibn al-Haytham_, 6.

p. 59, "true demonstrations . . ." Ibid.

p. 60, "true demonstrations relating . . ." Ibid.

p. 61, "the physicists . . . at face value," Ibid., 4.

p. 61-62, "Now, for any two . . ." Ibid., 5.

p. 62, "We should distinguish . . ." Ibid., 5–6.

p. 62-63, "the surface of . . . rulers and tubes," Ibid., 7.

p. 63, "If . . . he covers . . . surface of the eye," Ibid., 8.

p. 63, "Sight does not perceive . . . " Ibid.

p. 65, "The light shining . . . from that point," Ibid., 20.

p. 65-66, "a well-straightened . . . part of the fire," Ibid., 22.

p. 66, "From the light that . . ." Ibid.

p. 67, "an opening or door . . . light in the chamber," Ibid., 22.

p. 68, "it follows that these . . . " Ibid., 89.

p. 69, "all being opposite . . . to its place," Ibid., 90.

p. 69-70, "a chamber with . . . it has arrived," Ibid., 90–91.

p. 73, "the manner of vision generally," Ibid., 6.

p. 73, "the structure of the eye," Ibid., 3.

p. 74, "reflection from smooth . . . through transparent bodies," Ibid., 6.

CHAPTER SIX: Return to Basra

p. 76, "true demonstrations . . ." Ibn al-Haytham, *The Optics of Ibn al-Haytham*, 6.

p. 77, "the non-negotiable price," Sabra, Introduction to *The Optics of Ibn al-Haytham*, xx–xxi.

p. 79, "You deserve this . . . or a gift," Chaudhri, "Educational and Scientific Importance," 112.

p. 79, "All that I need . . ." Ibid.

p. 81, "dark chambers," Sabra, Introduction to *The Optics of Ibn al-Haytham*, vol. II, lii.

p. 81, "the form of the . . ." Ibid., li.

p. 82, "concepts whose matter . . ." Omar, *Ibn al-Hyatham's Optics*, 13.

p. 82, "the circumstances of . . . of intellected circles," Ibn al-Haytham, *On the Configuration of the World*, trans. Y. Tzvi Langermann (New York: Garland Publishing, 1990), 53.

p. 83, "The diameter of . . ." Y. Tzvi Langermann, Introduction to *Configuration of the World*, 8.

p. 84, "to the surfaces . . . possibly be consummated," Ibn al-Haytham, *Configuration of the World*, 53–54.

p. 84, "each of the motions . . ." Ibid., 55.

p. 84, "This is utter nonsense . . ." Langermann, Introduction to *Configuration of the World*, 9–10.

p. 84-85, "any hindrance . . . of a sphere," Ibn al-Haytham, *Configuration of the World*, 60.

p. 85-86, "The part surrounding . . . all these orbs," Ibid., 69.

p. 90, "Verily my return . . ." Chaudhri, "Educational and Scientific Importance," 123.

CHAPTER SEVEN: "The Physicist"

p. 91, "fallen into the hands . . ." Sabra, Introduction to *The Optics of Ibn al-Haytham*, vol. II, xxiv.

p. 92, "May God protect us . . ." A. I. Sabra, *Optics, Astronomy*

and Logic: Studies in Arabic Science and Philosophy
(Brookfield, Vermont: Variorum, 1994), 240.

p. 92, "The problems of physics . . ." Ibn Khaldun, _The Muqaddimah: An Introduction to History_, trans. Franz Rosenthal (Princeton: Princeton University Press, 1967), 251–252.

p. 92, "Philosophy was the foundation . . ." A. I. Sabra, "Problems of Scientific Borrowing: The Historical Background" in _Science and Technology in the Eastern Arab Countries_ (Princeton: Haskins Press, 1965), 11.

p. 96, "We believe in Allah . . ." _The Qur'an_, Chapter 2, verse 136.

p. 96, "He who wrongs . . ." _Encyclopaedia Britannica Online_ s.v. "Ahl al-Kitab," http://www.britannica.com/eb/article-9004124 (accessed January 14, 2006).

p. 102, "[Peregrinus] gains knowledge . . ." J. J. O'Connor and E. F. Robertson, "Roger Bacon," The MacTutor History of Mathematics archive, http://www-history.mcs.st-andrews.ac.uk/Mathematicians/Bacon.html (accessed June 21, 2006).

p. 112, "Our country must change . . ." Sabra, "Problems of Scientific Borrowing," 3.

p. 115-116, "Truth is sought...prejudice or leniency" "Critical Thinking Skills," The New England College of Optometry, http://www.neco.edu/library/PDF/OD2handout.pdf (accessed June 21, 2006).

bibliography

Chaudhri, Abdul Ghafur. "Ibn al-Haitham: The Educational and Scientific Importance of his Writings." In *Ibn al-Haitham, Proceedings of the Celebrations of 1000ʰ Anniversary*. Edited by Hakim Mohammed Said. Sadar, Pakistan: The Times Press, 1969.

Encyclopaedia Britannica Online. "Ahl al-Kitab." http://www. britannica.com/eb/article-9004124.

———. "Islam." http://www.britannica.com/eb/article-69166.

———. "One Thousand and One Nights." http://www.britannica .com/eb/article-907226.

Haque, Serajul, PhD. "A Peep into the Life and Works of Ibn al-Haitham." In *Ibn al-Haitham, Proceedings of the Celebrations of 1000ʰ Anniversary*. Edited by Hakim Mohammed Said. Sadar, Pakistan: The Times Press, 1969.

Hogendijk, J. P. *Ibn al-Haytham's* Completion of the Conics. New York: Springer-Verlag, 1985.

Ibn al-Haytham. *On the Configuration of the World*. Trans. Y. Tzvi Langermann. New York: Garland Publishing, 1990.

———. *The Optics of Ibn al-Haytham*. Trans. A. I. Sabra. London: The Warburg Institute, 1989.

Ibn Khaldun. *The Muqaddimah: An Introduction to History*. Trans. Franz Rosenthal. Princeton: Princeton University Press, 1967.

Lindberg, David C. *Studies in the History of Medieval Optics*. London: Variorum Reprints, 1983.

Nasir, Dr. Ahmad Naseer. "Ibn al-Haitham and His Philosophy." In *Ibn al-Haitham; Proceedings of the Celebrations of 1000ᵗʰ Anniversary*. Edited by Hakim Mohammed Said. Sadar, Pakistan: The Times Press, 1969.

The New England College of Optometry. "Critical Thinking Skills." http://www.neco.edu/library/PDF/OD2handout.pdf.

O'Connor, J. J., and E. F. Robertson. "Roger Bacon." The MacTutor History of Mathematics archive. http://www-history.mcs.st-andrews.ac.uk/Mathematicians/Bacon.html.

Omar, Saleh Beshara. *Ibn al-Hyatham's* Optics. Minneapolis: Bibliotheca Islamica, 1977.

Sabra, A. I., *Optics, Astronomy and Logic: Studies in Arabic Science and Philosophy*. Brookfield, Vermont: Variorum, 1994.

———. "Problems of Scientific Borrowing: The Historical Background." In *Science and Technology in the Eastern Arab Countries*. Princeton: Haskins Press, 1965.

———. *Theories of Light: from Descartes to Newton*. London: Oldbourne, 1967.

Sabra, Abdelhamid I., and Jan P. Hogendijk, eds. *The Enterprise of Science in Islam: New Perspectives*. Cambridge, Massachusetts: MIT Press, 2003.

Said, Hakim Mohammed, ed. *Ibn al-Haitham; Proceedings of the Celebrations of 1000ᵗʰ Anniversary*. Sadar, Pakistan: The Times Press, 1969.

Smith, A. Mark, ed. *Alhacen's Theory of Visual Perception*. Philadelphia: American Philosophical Society, 2001.

USC-MSA Compendium of Muslim Texts. "Ten Misconceptions about Islam." http://www.usc.edu/dept/MSA/notislam/misconceptions.html.

web sites

http://www.harvardmagazine.com/on-line/090351.html
An overview of Ibn al-Haytham's life and place in history by Abdelhamid I. Sabra, a translator of *The Book of Optics* and professor emeritus at Harvard University.

http://www.omarfoundation.org/Culture/History%20Science. htm
A detailed history of Muslim contributions to science between the eighth and eleventh centuries provided by the Omar Ibn Al Khattab Foundation in Los Angeles.

http://www.muslimheritage.com/day_life/default.cfm
Brief biographies of several important Muslim scholars with descriptions of their major contributions to learning.

http://www.pbs.org/empires/islam/index.html
An accompaniment to the PBS film *Islam: Empire of Faith*, this website features timelines and articles on Islamic faith, culture, innovations, and historical figures.

index

Abu Bakr, 28

Abu Hashim, 37

Abu Kamil, 20, 23

Alexander the Great, 33, 37

Al-Hakim Bi-amr Allah, 46,
    47-52, 54-55, 76, 87, 90

'Ali ('Ali Ibn Abi Talib), 28-
    30, 49

Al-Musabashshir ibn Fatik, 78

Apollonius of Perga, 14

Archimedes, 14, 37-38, 73

Aristotle, 14, 27, 32-34, 36-37,
    58, 61, 70-72, 98, 100, 102-
    103, 107

'Askari, Ahmad ibn Muhammad
    ibn Ja'far al-, 40, 88, 111

'Attar, Hasan al-, 112

Bacon, Roger, 100-103

Bayhaqi, 'Ali ibn Zayd al-, 42,
    50-52, 54-55, 79, 87, 90

Bonaparte, Napoleon, 112-
    113, *113*

Brahe, Tycho, 106, 108

Copernicus, Nico-
    laus, 86, 106,
    108, 111

Euclid, 14, 37, 58, 61, 77,
    98, 103

Galen, 14, 73, 98

Galilei, Gali-
    leo, 86, 107, 109-
    111, *110*

Gerard of Cremona, 97-
98

Ghiberti, Lorenzo, 104-
105

Hasan, 28, *29*

Hevelius, Johannes, 109-
    110

Husayn, 28-30, *29*

Hussein, Saddam, 114-
115

Huygens, Christian, 109

Ibn al-Haytham, Abu 'Ali al-
  Hasan ibn al-Hasan, *10,*
  110, 115
  birth, 12
  death, 90
  works,
      Book of Optics, 40,
      57-75, *59, 74,* 80-81,
      88,90,91,98-107,109,
      111-112
      Completion of the
      Conics of Apollonius,
      112
      Determination of the
      Altitudes of Mountains,
      41
      Determination of the
      Height of The Pole. . .
      Precision, 41
      Discourse on Light, 81
      Doubts Concerning
      Ptolemy, 80, 83, 108,
      116
      On the Altitudes of
      Triangles, 41
      On Business Arithme-
      tic, 41
      On the Configuration
      of the World, 82, 86,
      108-109, 112
      On the Construction of
      the Water Clock, 41
      On the Principles of
      Measurement, 41
      A Reply by [Ibn al-
      Haythem] to a Geo-
      metrical Question . . .
      A.H. *418,* 87
      Replies to Seven Math-
      ematical Questions. . .
      Baghdad, 24, 87
      Treatise on the Appear-
      ance of Stars, 81
      Treatise on the Burning
      Sphere, 82
      Treatise on the Form
      of the Eclipse, 81
      Treatise on the Light
      of the Moon, 81
      Treatise on the Lights
      of the Stars, 81
      Treatise on Parabolic
      Burning Mirrors, 82,
      98
      Treatise on Spherical
      Burning Mirrors, 82
      Treatise on the Rain-
      bow and the Halo, 81
      Treatise on What Ap-
      pears of the Differences
      of the Heights of the
      Stars, 81

Ibn Khaldum, 92
Ibn al-Shatir, 95
Ibn Yunus, 47

Ibn Yunus, Ishaq, 79

Jashyari, Abu 'Abd Allah ibn
    'Abdus al-, 17-18
ben Judah, Joseph, 77-78
Kepler, Johannes, 75, 86, 107-
    109, 111
Khattab, Umar ibn al-,22
Khwarizmi, Muhammad ibn
    Musa al-, 19-21, 23, 96
Kindi, Ya'qub ibn Ishaq as-
    Sabah al-, 58, 70-72, 96

Maimonides, Moses, 93, *93*
Ma'mun, al- (Abu Jafar al-
    Ma'mun ibn Harun), 14-15,
    98
Mu'awiyah, 28
Muhammed 'Ali, 112
Muhammad, Prophet, 12-14,
    22-23, 26, 28-29, *29*, 47,
    49, 92, 96

Nahhavi, Yahya, 36
Newton, Isaac, 109

Pecham, John, 103-104
Peregrinus, Peter, 100, 102-
    103
Plato, 14, 33,
Ptolemy, 14, 16-17, 38, 58,
    61, 73, 75, 77-78, 80, 82-84,
    97, 103

Qaysar, 39-41, 44
Qifti, Jamal al-Din ibn al-, 50,
    52, 54-55, 60, 76-77, 87

Riccioli, Gianbattista, 111
Risner, Frederick, 105-106

Surkhab, 79

Tabari, Sahl ibn Rabban al-,
    16
Tahtawi, Rifa 'a Rafi al-, 112
Theon of Alexandria, 58,
    70-72

Usaybi'ah (Ibn Abi Usaybi'ah),
    39, 42, 78, 80-81, 87, 91

William of Moerbeke, 103
Witelo, Erazmus Ciolek, 103-
    104

Yazid, 28, 30